The Wor[ld is Full of]
Laughter

'This book started as a
possible suicide note and
ended up a celebration
of life.'
Dolly Sen

'This book will save lives'
Jason Pegler

www.chipmunkapublishing.com

Published by
Chipmunkapublishing,
PO Box 6872
Brentwood,
Essex CM13 1ZT
United Kingdom

Copyright © 2002 D Sen and Chipmunkapublishing
Cover designed by Isaac Quaye

A record of this book is in the British Library
ISBN 0 9542218 1 8
Printed and bound in Great Britain

For Dad,
With lots of love, some
peace, and a little bit of pain.

ACKNOWLEDGMENTS

My thanks to Jason Pegler, author of 'A Can of Madness' for inspiring me to write this memoir; to the members of my family who laughed at the pain with me; to Judith Johnson; to Doctor Thomson, Doctor Masterton, Rachel Murray, Chris Hart and Nadir Mothojakan for being human before being professionals; to all at First Step Trust, especially Stuart Mckee; to Charles Bukowski, Henry Rollins and Jack Kerouac for teaching me that I can write my life any way I like; to the Buddha, thanks for the instruction manual; and finally to my parents, thank you for giving me life.

ACKNOWLEDGEMENTS

Foreword

'The World Is Full Of Laughter' is a gripping tale of a woman's fight to come to terms with abuse, family pressures, prejudice and mental ill health. Dolly describes the reality and prejudices of being diagnosed with various psychiatric conditions. Add this to a series of horrific experiences in her life, and it is remarkable how she has the strength to come through events with such vigour, optimism and warmness.

Dolly Sen's memoirs describe what it is like to be a mental health survivor looking in on the rest of society. She writes with lucidity and clarity of thought. The narrative flows in an entertaining fashion, with a charming sense of irony.

I will always remember how I felt when I finished reading the book. There was a tear resting on my right cheek for half an hour. This book will save lives.

Jason Pegler
Author of A Can Of Madness and founder of Chipmunkapublishing.

Prologue

'The human being... is a book reading itself.'

P.N. Furbank on Diderot

I'm self-hate surrounded by mirrors.

Not the many glass ones I have shattered, ensuring I have no good luck for the next thousand lifetimes. No, the mirror of the eyes that constantly watch me. Mirrors with names, smiles, souls and lies.

"You've got your Daddy's eyes and your Daddy's lies. Cut them out!" The voices tell me over and over again.

Can memories turn into psychosis? These are memories that touch me with the insistence of a branding iron. Writing this memoir, I have to make sure that it doesn't turn into a suicide note.

My father was an actor and musician, so I grew up in the entertainment industry. My father also thought of himself as a comedian, but you didn't hear much laughter in our home.

The first film I remember working in as an extra was 'The Empire Strikes Back'. The film set was the interior of a space station and there were all kinds of monsters walking about. I didn't know it was make-believe – I thought it was a documentary. 20 years later my mind had left planet Earth too.

"You've got your Daddy's eyes and your Daddy's lies. Cut them out!"

I'm standing over my sleeping father with a knife in my hand. Because he is a demonic alien plotting my destruction, he has to die; I am going to bring down the knife down on his face. "Look who's laughing now," I say. It doesn't matter to me that I am heading for a special hospital or eventual suicide. As a mental health professional said to me: "Dolly, your next stop is Broadmoor." It didn't matter because I did what I had to do to survive. Can't people understand that?

As he sleeps, I watch him, waiting for the right moment to kill. Waiting. Waiting. His awful body odour, the old food in his beard, the spit marks on the floor, just makes me angrier and angrier. I raise the knife, ready to plunge it into this fucking waste of a human being. Another set of eyes is staring at me - from the wall. It is a picture of me as a child, smiling for the camera. I try three times to stab my father's skull, but a child is watching, and I can't do it. "I'm sorry for turning you into a murderer," I say to the photo. "I used to be a child once, I used to be a little girl…

PART ONE

A little girl

My parents met in a pub in Victoria station during the summer of 1968. My Mum was signing to her friend who was also deaf, and the friend kept nudging her, saying, "That handsome Indian guy at the bar keeps looking at me!"

He wasn't looking at the friend but at my Mum, a 21-year-old Scots girl who had recently moved to London. She was dressed like a hippy, with a bandana holding up her fiery red hair and accentuating her green eyes. My Mum showed me a picture of her taken during this time. She looked a bit like Janis Joplin. My father, on the other hand, looked like an Indian Elvis Presley. If anybody ever wondered what the offspring of Janis Joplin and Elvis would look like, they just have to check out my siblings and me.

My Dad came over to their table and asked them what was the sign language for 'Would you like a drink?' They taught him. 'Would you like a drink?' he signed clumsily. They both said yes.

He explained to them he was waiting for a friend who didn't turn up. "What's your name?" My father mouthed slowly to my mother, ignoring her friend. "Heather," she said.

"That's a nice name. My name is Egbert, but people call me Chicko because I'm very cheeky." He grinned.

Chicko and Heather went out together on and off for a couple of years. He got her a job in the same office as him as a stock clerk for the department store Barkers. He also had a job at the weekend playing Indian music for the BBC's first Asian TV show. There was one story about that time he is fond of relaying. Princess Margaret was a customer and she was late settling her account. My father wrote her office a harsh letter and they in turn complained to the store. He had his hand slapped for that. But he was always proud he gave a member of royalty a telling off.

During the spring of 1970 my Mum found out she was pregnant with me. She didn't know how to tell my father. He had never hit her but he did have a temper on him. Plus she knew his family bitterly disapproved of their inter-racial relationship. My Dad's reaction was to blow his top and refuse to see my mother ever again. "This will ruin my life." And he walked away from her. But something made him pause in his step and he turned around to look at my Mum. She was crying and looked so alone. Who would care for a pregnant deaf woman, he thought. He walked back to my mother. "That was the worst mistake of my life." He was fond of telling me.

They were married soon after at a registry office, my Mum wearing a sari and Indian jewellery and my Dad in an English suit. The only person at that time in his family who was friendly to my mother was my father's younger brother, nicknamed Baba. He was best man.

11

I was born in Mile End Hospital in Stepney, within the sound of Bow bells. As I was almost 2 weeks late, they induced the birth. The weeks prior to the birth I had been in the breach position, which finally corrected itself. The doctor told my Mum, "This kid doesn't want to be born."

After an 8-hour labour, a newly qualified doctor delivered me into the world. Cutting my umbilical cord, he accidentally nicked my stomach with his scalpel. I still bear the scar now.

My Dad has spent the labour in a pub, telling everybody he was going to have a son to carry on his name. He had left his job at the department store to concentrate on his music. When he finally staggered onto the ward, a nurse told him he had a girl. "A girl! There's already too many girls in the family." But his disappointment melted when he saw me, he said. I stuck my tongue out at him.

The woman in the next bed was glued to the TV screen. Her husband was a policeman and there were racial riots on the day I was born. Her husband finally burst into the ward in riot gear, running over to his wife to give her a hug. He woke me up.

A nun at the hospital took a shine to me. She told my Mum I was the loudest crying baby, but also the one who smiled the most. She took me off my Mum's hands and wouldn't be seen for hours.

I stayed in hospital longer than usual because I developed jaundice and refused to eat. I dropped from 6lb 12oz to just over 5lbs. But the jaundice passed and I regained my appetite and soon left the hospital. I was named Dolly Norah Sen, after both my dead grandmothers.

We stayed in the East End until I was a year old. We lived in a small mouse-infested room on Brick Lane. My parents began arguing more often because my Dad would be out all day and spend what little money they had on drinks, sometimes leaving my Mum without food. My mother knew my father liked his drink, but this was something new for her. It was as if life became something to hide from now that I was born. My Mum's only friend was the wife of an associate of the Krays. She made sure me and Mum didn't go hungry, and told my Dad off whenever she saw him. My father also had a passing acquaintance with a few East End gangsters and he exploited this to his advantage a few times. For example, he was barred from one pub because of his colour; so a few heavies went to the pub and threw a few things about.

He would also wheel my pram into a gangster pub. The patrons there never failed to fill my pram with money, sometimes up to £50, which was a lot of money in those days. My Dad gave a few quid to my Mum, and kept the rest for himself.

During my teething period, my father hung me out the window by a leg, threatening to drop me because I wouldn't stop crying. My father was particularly proud of that story when I was older.

My father's family soon came round and accepted my Mum and me into the family. They had found a flat near them in Streatham, South London, and invited us to live there and be close to the family. My father accepted, but that didn't work out because he had an argument with the landlord and my parents returned from a trip to find all their belongings on the street outside. So they went to Lambeth council's homeless unit and were placed in temporary accommodation for a month before they were offered a spacious council flat in Streatham.

Streatham was once a Roman settlement, and then it became a rural Surrey village. During my lifetime it went from a middle class, primarily white suburb to a multi-cultural sidebite of the metropolis. This change has been reflected in my accent. I used to have quite a posh accent. Then the inner city sneaked up on Streatham in the 80s, and as a consequence I developed a strong 'Sarf' London accent, which I have now. But I can return to my posh accent when the need arises, usually when I have to make a phone call. Now in 2002 a lot of young professional couples are moving into the area and the town teetering towards being middle class again

Our new home was a stone's throw from Streatham Common and had quite a history and a lot of character. It was part of a large building which used to be a convent, hence its name – Coventry Hall. There was supposed to be a ghostly nun haunting the building. Most of the adults didn't see it and those that did were sent to the local Tooting Bec insane asylum. Almost all the kids saw it, including me, although I don't remember it. My Mum saw me talking to an empty space. 'Whom are you talking too?' she asked. "Nun. Nun." I replied. It was a nice place; plenty of room to run about, but it was always overrun by mice. I found a couple in my cot once feasting on a discarded biscuit. Coventry Hall was eventually knocked down a decade later and replaced by a housing office. I don't know if the ghost is still there.

In my terrible twos, I threw the loudest screaming tantrums on this side of the hemisphere. My father's slaps to my body got harder and harder but he was unable to shut me up. They had to bribe me into shutting up by buying me sweets and toys. Or if we were at the pub my Dad would give me some of his Guinness. Every time he poured a glass, he let me suck up the frothing head – that was the only part I liked. I was also a tenacious little thing. During a shopping trip I insisted I carried home a 2-litre bottle of orange juice, which was almost the same height as me. My parents kept offering to take it off my hands but I screamed every time they tried. They said the 5-minute walk home took half an hour.

Toys only lasted a few days before I broke them to see what was inside. My parents bought me a toy replica of a bus conductor's ticket machine. On the bus I followed the real bus conductor around issuing tickets to passengers from my machine in exchange for sweets. "Ah, ain't she cute!" said one passenger.

Once I got home however I wanted to see how the machine worked, so I broke it open, much to the despair of my parents. My Dad just seemed to get angrier and angrier as the days went on. I did that to all my toys. I hated dolls; I always took their heads off or scribbled over their faces. They finally did find a toy that lasted longer than a few days, and that was Lego, because you can't really take it apart but only build with it.

My Mum brought home a different doll one day. This one has skin like me and cried a lot. I was told this was my new sister, Sheila. I was no longer allowed to sleep in the cot; it was Sheila's now. I didn't like this at all and slapped the baby. My Dad slapped me hard around the legs to tell me slapping was wrong. If Sheila was picked up, I wanted to be picked up too. Sheila's incessant crying and rocking back and forth as a year old stressed my father to breaking point. He began beating my mother. At 18 months old Sheila began complaining of headaches and was losing the feeling and use of her left side. My Mum's social worker for the deaf arranged for Sheila to be seen at the Maudsley Hospital. An X-ray revealed a tumour in my sister's brainstem. The doctors said they had to operate straight away to remove it.

Going to and from the hospital without much rest made my mother lose a lot of weight, so it was decided she would stay at the hospital with Sheila, and my Dad would look after me. I liked it at the hospital; it was there I made my first friends. On a free reign on my sister's ward, usually I just ran up and down the ward, but sometimes strange-looking children stopped me in my tracks. There was one kid with water on the brain whom I thought was an alien. The ward comprised of a dormitory of beds with single rooms at each end. In one of these rooms was the first friend I made. He was a Greek lad but spoke English. His parents could only speak Greek. I would sit on his bed and, on one large piece of paper we would draw and scribble, or assemble wooden puzzles.

One morning after I played with my sister for a little while, I ran to the end of the ward to see my Greek friend, I can't recall his name. I ran into his room: his bed was empty, his parents were packing away his things and crying hysterically. I asked them where he was. His mother couldn't even look at me. I left the room and asked a nurse what happened to my friend.

"He's gone to heaven, sweetie."

"Heaven is nice, isn't it? Why is his Mum sad?"

"Come on, Dolly, I'll take you back to your Mum."

There was a boy on the ward, directly opposite my sister, who had both his legs in plaster. I don't remember why we hated each other but we did. He would always try and make fun of me and get the other kids to steal my only toy – a ladybug on small wheels. Mum told me I smacked him once but I don't remember that, but I do remember him deciding to enlighten me about my Greek friend. "He's dead, stupid."

"Dead?"

"He's gone to sleep and he'll never wake up. They are going to put him in a box and bury him in the ground."

I began to sob. "No, no, why is that?"

"Because you're stupid."

I asked my Dad, "Why did my friend die?"

"Because he just did."

Tears welled up.

"Shut up, Dolly! SHUT UP!"

"Is Sheila going to die?"

He slapped my legs out from under me. "Don't say that!"

"But is she going to die?"

"If you be quiet and good, God will save her."

I tried my best to be good but when you're 4... well, you're 4. Returning to our flat in Coventry Hall one night, I saw who I thought was my Mum in the fish and chip shop. I wanted to go in there and hug my Mum.

"That's not you're fucking Mum, stupid!"

"No, Mummy, Mummy!" I pulled him towards the fish and chip shop. My Dad picked me up and carried me away from the shop. I was inconsolable. My Dad was shaking me to stop crying. By now I was screaming. In the end my Dad found a way to shut me up. "If you don't shut up, Sheila will die, and it'll be all your fault!"

I was still crying but softly now. "Mummy," I mouthed.

When you're 4 you believe in monsters. They come out at night and take pieces of your soul. My Dad would make me go to bed early even if I wasn't tired. There were no lullabies, just obscenities. When he thought I was asleep, he'd leave the flat to go drinking, leaving me alone. I was too scared to sleep and too scared to stay awake. Ever since my friend died, I had trouble sleeping because I thought I wasn't going to wake up again. But sometimes death is preferable when the 1001 monsters of the surrounding dark surround you for hours and hours on end. But the worst monster would come staggering through the door, steaming drunk and swearing and slurring. The longer Sheila spent in hospital, the more he spent on drink

One time there was no money for our bus fare to the hospital, so we had to walk there, and it is a good few miles. Dad always told this story to all his children as proof that he did care for us; otherwise he wouldn't have walked so far to see Sheila. He couldn't see the joke he became; that because of his alcoholism, there was no money for the bus and he forced a young child to walk so far; and two, that he could count those stories on one hand, the hand that beat the shit out of us. It was clear to all my father couldn't cope with me so I went to stay at his siblings' house, where I was spoilt rotten by my aunts and uncles. My Uncle Baba worked as a security guard at the National Gallery and he had this walk there I remember as he ambled from gallery to gallery telling me about the paintings: pacing slowly up and down with his hands behind his back. He would do this in his hallway and I would be right behind him, aping his actions, a mini security guard.

Meanwhile, the doctors decided to operate on Sheila and remove the tumour from her brainstem. I saw her on the day after the op. Her head was shaven, and she had a metal clip in the back of her head, instead of stitches. I gave her a hug and was told off for doing that. "Be careful," everybody said to me. Sheila had to learn to talk and walk again, and regain the use of her left side. I played my part in do this by offering her a sweetie and not giving it to her unless she used her left hand to take it. Soon she was up and running around with me. I was glad she didn't die and we became inseparable after that. Whenever somebody made fun of her baldhead or operation scar, I would thump him or her with my tiny fists.

Having a child that had been seriously ill drove my father over the edge and he became a full-fledged alcoholic. He didn't care about anything, not even his music. He gained a reputation of getting into arguments at the gigs he played at, and people hired him less and less. The more he drank, the more violent he became. He beat Mum so badly she lost the baby she was carrying on Christmas Day. My little body also absorbed his punches. I went from being boisterous and energetic to being passive and shy with a bed-wetting problem. This state of being was helped along by a serious accident I had: Sheila and I were running about and I knocked over the paraffin heater boiling some milk. The hot liquid scalded my right lower leg, taking the skin off. I went to St George's Hospital to be treated. I fought violently with the nurses holding me down to clean up my leg. My Dad told me a nurse said, "I didn't know a little thing could cause so much pain." I was beginning to understand pain.

The drinking took its toil on Dad's body and he suffered a severe abdominal haemorrhage soon after, which had to be operated upon. To this day he doesn't blame it on the drinking. "It's that bloody Lemsip I drank that did this!"

Once again my aunts and uncles looked me after - this time with Sheila too. They took us to Windsor Safari Park, where we were frightened half to tears by the monkeys tearing off the windscreen wipers on my uncle's car. When we visited our Dad in hospital we also saw my Dad's aunt whom I called grapefruit because she would always give me one whenever I saw her. She admonished my Dad for drinking and told me, "He's always been a naughty boy."

My father was born in Bombay, India in 1932 or 1934; my grandfather was unable to quite remember which. He was the second child of 6 and the second son of Dr Lawrence Sen and Dr Dolly Sen. My grandfather a pharmacist, my grandmother a gynaecologist. She earned more than he did but my grandfather was definitely the head of the family. My grandma was part Nepalese and very committed Christian. She was a kind woman, she would charge people for delivering babies according to their means, and if they couldn't afford it, she wouldn't charge at all. Or people would give her goods instead of money. One time she came home with a baby whose parents were unable to look after him. So she adopted him. My grandfather, however, was a strict disciplinarian, and it was usually my Dad who got the brunt of his beatings;

he was definitely the naughtiest child – fighting, stealing, truanting, and drinking at 15. When my father beat us, he said, "My father beat me as a child and I turned out okay." Irony is a thing a child should really not learn.

His mother had to pay someone off not to hurt him for double-crossing some kind of crook. One of my favourite stories about my father's time in India was when a man came to my father's house threatening to kill him for stealing his money. My father was with his Aunt Bella, my grandfather's sister. She spent her days sitting outside her house, chain-smoking. She was a butch woman and acted like a man. My father explained to his aunt that this man was going to hurt him. So she charged straight into this man and beat the shit out of him! She did the same for others. The kids in the neighbourhood loved her; they knew she'd always protect them. I would have loved to meet her, but she died many years before I was born. I think I inherited some of her character however. I definitely am and love being a woman, but I definitely have a masculine energy about me, and I feel it's up to me to protect those around me.

Anyway, my father disclosed to me that he *had* stolen the man's money!

I asked my father one time why he got into so much trouble. "I was bored," is the best he can come up with. He also said another time he was angry with his father for ignoring him and wanted to punish him by embarrassing him. I think that is true, but on another level I think he also sought attention and affection from his father. And now at the age of 70 he is still seeking attention from a father that has been dead and buried for some years. I believe he doesn't know how to stop or what to do instead.

Growing up, my father found something he was good at. He became a very accomplished Indian musician and singer. He thought he father would be proud of him, but instead his father was disgusted and disappointed, thinking it was a disgraceful profession, full of drunks and druggies. It was - but that was beside the point. My father had a genuine talent but his father refused to acknowledge it. It hurt my father deeply and he only felt good when he was drinking or making music. My father decided to emigrate to the UK to start a new life in 1957.

He took the ship route to Liverpool, seasick and homesick. He missed his Mum terribly, crying for her every night. Once in England, he travelled about a bit before settling in Streatham with his siblings. They were one of the first Indian people to live in the area and were at the receiving end of a few racist attacks: my Dad had to save his brother from being beaten up by a group of teddy boys. In 1959 his mother died of thyroid cancer. This devastated him. His family said he wasn't the same after that, his drinking and partying got harder and harder. Even now he cries like a baby every time the subject of his mother is brought up.

During the day my Dad worked in a variety of stock keeping jobs; at night he played in clubs with the band he fronted as singer and harmonium (an Indian small piano) player. As he often boasted, he was the first person to introduce popular Indian music to the UK. At one of his shows he met an agent who signed him up to work in films. At first he arranged musical scores for films and then began acting. He played some Indian music in The Beatles film 'HELP', where he said he had an argument with Ringo Starr about who was the better drummer. Because of this status he was never short of girlfriends. "I could have been with any woman I liked, but instead I ended up with your bitch mother. And if it weren't for *you*" he'd point at me, "I'd be rich and famous by now."

My mother was born Heather Milton in Motherwell, Scotland in March 1947. There's quite a big age gap between my Mum and her two older siblings, Mary and Freddy, because her father was away fighting in the 2nd World War. She was born hearing. At age 2 she contracted measles along with her younger sister Ellen. They both became very ill - my Mum almost didn't make it. Unfortunately the disease left her deaf.

Her father Edward Milton was a down-to-earth, solid man. He had no time for my Dad's airy-fairy pretensions, and told him so. There was always a palpable tension whenever my Dad and granddad were together. He worked in Ravenscraig, the local steel mill. The work was hot and dirty and his wife would have to take out the steel splinters that became embedded in his legs. It seems to me looking at photos of my mother as a child, my grandfather had always been bald, although I'm sure this is not the case. He told his children stories about the war as an artillery soldier, about being

24

attacked by a monkey in the Far East and seeing a shrunken head in Africa, and losing good friends. He had tattoos on his arms, one of my dead grandmother. My Mum tells me they were poor but happy. They never went hungry with their Mum's great homely cooking.

Her Mum, Margaret O'Dwyer, was born in Dublin, Ireland, but everybody called her Norah. She moved to Newcastle as a child, and later on to Scotland, where she met my granddad. I don't know too much about her past but hers wasn't happy childhood. My grandmother's stepmother wasn't welcomed into the family because of this. My grandmother trained as a nurse was as kind as my grandmother on my father's side. I think they knew each other in a former life. My Mum was her favourite and spoilt rotten and sheltered. My gran loved a good gossip and would read the neighbour's tealeaves for them. She died one day before my mother's 18th birthday. My grandmother was unable to recognise her family the last time they saw her. Thinking about this still upsets my mother. To this day Mum doesn't know exactly what killed her mother. She just doesn't like to bring the subject up with her family for some reason.

Her schooling was pretty horrific. The teachers were more interested in punishing her for being deaf than providing a useful education. My Mum one time had to wear headphones and raise her hand every time she heard a beep. Being profoundly deaf, her hand stayed down. And because of this had her knuckles rapped by a ruler. Anybody with nits had their head shaved in front of the class like a sheep. They were in the same class from infancy to the day they left school. Mum was happy to leave.

She found a job, first in a butcher shop, then as a machinist for a garments factory. Her three other siblings had emigrated to Australia and Canada to start new lives. My Mum lost her job, and one by one her friends married and moved away. She wanted a new life too. She didn't have the means to go abroad so she went with a friend to try her luck in London. She and her friend quickly found lodgings and jobs. Every Friday they would unwind with a drink at the pub in Victoria Station...

After his op, Dad stayed off the drink for a little while at the request of his doctors. But he decided he knew more than them. "All the people that told me to stop drinking, all died in their 40s and 50s. God is on my side. I'll be okay."

My Mum's social worker thought otherwise. She thought someone who nearly died because of their alcohol abuse and carried on drinking regardless had to be mentally ill. This conviction was compounded by my father's grandiose insistence he was more talented than anyone on the planet. The social worker decided my Mum was mentally ill on the grounds she was deaf and therefore an inadequate mother and that she thought the world was laughing at her. The world *was* laughing at her, thanks to my father's putdowns. He would do anything for a laugh. So what if he constantly humiliated my mother – couldn't she take a joke?

Whilst they were being assessed in a psychiatric hospital in Preston, Sheila and I were looked after by foster parents. All I remember of that time is that the foster mum taught me how to use a potter's wheel and helped me make a very unformed pot, which I was proud of. When my parents were discharged from hospital, I gave the pot to my Dad to cheer him up. "What do I want with a fucking rubbish thing like that?" It became an ashtray. My Dad had told the psychiatrists, "Stop asking me fucking stupid questions, I could do your job better than you. Who do you think you are?" I guess this is the voice of sanity because my parents were given a clean bill of health. Fucking crazy if you ask me…

Sheila and I then went to a pre-school nursery that overlooked Tooting Bec Common, I think to give my father more time to make more children to hate. My memory of that time is very sketchy but a few things do stand out. I remember the Disney characters painted on the windows. One time when we went into the back garden to play, we were told not to use the slide because it had been rainy and the bottom of the slide was muddy. Guess who ignored the warning and became mud-child.

One day a week we would have a slice of meat pate as part of our lunch. I still remember the smell of the meat pate to this day. Whenever I smell it as an adult it stops me in my tracks and I become a 3-year-old child again. There was a recurring dream I had back then which I still occasionally have now. It is of me in the middle of an immense field of golden flowers and haunting sunlight, and an angel is

27

beckoning me to follow her. I do and this always leads me to an even bigger field of gold. There have been times when close to suicide or death, that dream has replayed in my head. What is the significance of that, I don't know, but the dream always brings me a sense of peace. It is a dream without age; I don't feel like a child or adult in it, I feel eternal. What a beautiful strange feeling.

Sometimes when the weather was good we were taken to Tooting Bec Common to play and explore. The common was also used by day-release psychiatric patients who lived in an old Victorian Mental Hospital facing the other end of the common. We were warned by our nursery teachers not to go near these mad people. "They might hurt you." Despite the word of warning, I was intrigued by these people who babbled strange things and said they could see God, I don't know why. Maybe my life then realised this was where I was heading.

There was this old guy with a grey straggly beard who would give me a sweet if I spelt a 4 or 5-letter word correctly. My teachers were always telling me off for running up to this man to be tested on my spelling. My Dad found out about this and gave me a few slaps and kicks. "These people are dangerous! Stay away from them! They might hurt you!" Nonetheless he paved the happy way to my own psychosis.

To be a good comedian you need to understand irony, I think. And my Dad couldn't see the irony of attempting to protect us from an evil, harmful world of strangers by beating into us this fact in our home sweet home. Torture chambers have cushions and lampshades, TVs and welcome mats. He saw no discrepancy in wrapping us up in cotton wool just to soak up the blood he made us shed. I learnt what irony was from him at a very early age when he hammered our heads with a 'WORLD'S GREATEST DAD' plate he swiped off the wall – one *he* bought and put pride of place some months before.

With another baby on the way, we moved to a bigger place, a 3-bedroom red-bricked Maisonette on Keymer Road in Streatham. We had the top two floors; the ground floor belonged to an old white-haired man. The first floor housed two small bedrooms, a living room, a kitchen, a bathroom and the door to the garden. Up the curving stairs and you'd be in the main bedroom, which took up most of the top floor. It had one large round window that looked over the road and immensities of sky. There were also two attic-like rooms we kids named the 'dark room' where we were sure 1001 sprites and goblins lived, only to come out when we were asleep. It didn't take us long to realise the light has bigger demons.

Kenny was soon born in December 1974, finally the son my father wanted. When he heard the news over the telephone, Dad screamed and jumped around like a drugged-up kangaroo. He immediately went to the local pub, The John Company, to celebrate, dragging along Sheila and me. He dumped us outside the pub in the freezing cold and went inside to drink himself stupid. We didn't see him for I don't know how many hours, but it felt like days. In his haste to drown out a beautiful moment in the piss of alcohol, he forgot to put coats on Sheila and me. We were so cold outside the pub, we wanted to cry, and I think we did. "I should win father of the year!" he would say about fathering a son.

Mum was changing Kenny's nappy when we went to see the family's new arrival the next day. "Ahh, my son," my father cooed over the baby. Kenny pissed in his face. At his christening not long after, Kenny would scream, "Wah Wah Wah!" in the tone of 'get your damn hands off me' every time someone tried to pick him up. I was beginning to like my brother.

We all shared the bedroom on the top floor at first. Sheila and I had to go to bed at 7pm. If I crept down the stairs into the living room, complaining I was unable to sleep, I was dragged up the stairs by the scruff of my neck by my Dad. In a more benevolent mood he would tell Sheila and I bedtime stories about scary monkeymen who ate the brains of children who wouldn't sleep when they were told. Sheila and I dived under the covers of the bed we shared, too scared to breathe. When I was brave enough to come up for air, I always checked there were no monkeymen looking in through the window.

These happy stories contributed to my bed-wetting and sleepwalking, no doubt. My Dad's way in dealing with my bed-wetting was to show the neighbours my soiled sheets, saying, "Look, she still wets the bed! What did I do to deserve her?"

Dad only worked intermittently as a musician and actor, so if he was not at the pub, he stayed home for most of the day. I liked it when he did go to work. We had the freedom then to play and watch TV without being screamed at for annoying our Dad with our existence. Ordinarily our diet was pretty bland, but Dad would come back from film work with Kentucky Fried Chicken or McDonalds, we would crowd him as he came from the door, eagerly waiting for our treat.

But as time went on he was frustrated with only being a TV and film extra. He was angry the world didn't realise how great he was. He was always in a rage, and looking at his family only increased his rage. Can you understand that feeling? Of inducing disgust in another person. You realise it's better not to be seen at all.

Our Dad wouldn't let us play with the neighbourhood children. If somebody knocked to ask us to play, Dad told us to hide and not make a sound while he went downstairs to send the kids away. We were not allowed to have friends. Friends dirtied the soul. "The world is full of bad people," Dad told us, "I'm here to save you." So Dad kept us away from the cruel world outside to show us the cruel world inside was sufficient enough. I looked out the window and watched the children of the neighbourhood play – only for a short while, mind you. It was just too painful. There were stories at the time that UFOs were visiting Streatham. My Mum insisted she saw one flash across the sky above our street. At bedtime, just before sleep, I waited for an alien spacecraft to take me away, to take me **home,** wherever that was. I also began daydreaming about death and how wonderful it would be, because it would be mine and mine alone, my father couldn't own it, no matter how hard he tried, and boy did he try.

We couldn't even play at home most of the time. The old man downstairs complained we ran too much. So we got the message, not only from our Dad that we weren't allowed to be children. Which was okay, I guess. Since nobody ever asked me to be one, I was never really any good at being a child.

But I did manage to find ways to entertain myself, thanks to the TV. I rode motorcycles with Evil Kenevil, I crashed though boxes and plates of glass with Starksy and Hutch. After watching a film about a convict escaping from jail by digging through the wall, I ran to the kitchen for a spoon. An hour later there was a nice little hole in the living room wall about the size of an egg. I was still digging when my Dad entered the room, pissed. "What the fuck are you doing? You stupid bitch!" I couldn't see what he was so mad about, especially as he made the hole bigger by slamming my head against the crumbling plaster. Where was my Mum when all this was happening? Her reaction to my father's abuse didn't change for over 28 years: she screamed and cried at the top of voice, and that was all; it didn't go any further. My parents never talked about it and discussed things. To be honest, I have reservations that they ever had a conversation. Dad ordered us to do something and we did it. One time Dad hit Mum so hard he knocked her out. I thought she was dead. Dad looked at us staring at our Mum. "She's only playing. Laugh, you fuckers! Laugh!" And we did. We laughed at Dad, the comedian.

The very next day I watched another movie, this time about a safe blower. I memorised his technique. During the commercial break, I stuck a piece of modelling clay onto the wall; that was my plastic explosive. A piece of string was the fuse, a tissue box a detonator. Sheila and Kenny were my fellow crooks. I told them to be deadly quiet or the cops would get us. Sheila's eyes grew with fear; Kenny squealed with delight. "Ready? One…two…three… BOOM!" I bellowed. Sheila started crying. Kenny started laughing.

At the tender age of 5, my father decided I needed to pull my weight about the house. So I became my Mum's helper, assisting her with laundry, cleaning, and babysitting. I liked helping her in the garden. We planted carrots, peas and tomatoes; I loved watching them grow, even if they did come out malformed. There was a washing line between two metal poles. I climbed on the dustbin to slide down these poles like a fire fighter. We were allowed to play in the garden, so I loved going out there. It was a scrubby little thing with a concrete path directly down the middle, with a couple of rose bushes and a puny vegetable garden. Most of our neighbours disliked us: we were either too loud or too brown. Behind the tall brown fence lived a man with a dark moustache us kids nicknamed 'Bad man'. Kenny couldn't pronounce that and called him 'Batman' instead. If our ball went over the fence into his garden, we never got it back. "It's going straight in the bin!" he'd growl. Or he'd say, "Mixed breeds, fucking mongrels, your parents breed like rabbits. You don't belong here. You don't belong anywhere! Go back to where you came from!" And I don't think he meant back inside the house.

But directly opposite us lived a husband and wife who owned an ice cream machine. In the summer, if they were out in the garden, they'd always give us one cone each of dripping soft ice cream. I'd be disappointed if they weren't out in their garden. Sometimes I coughed loudly in the hopes of attracting their attention; it never worked though. I looked forward for days to having that ice cream.

Ken may have been the son he wanted, but he soon got bored of that, he saw all his children as an intrusion, an annoyance. Yet I felt he singled me out for harsher punishment, and my Mum bears this out. "It's all your fault." He'd say. "If it weren't for you, I would have gone far."

"I didn't ask to be born," I'd counter. Can you believe it? My father was angry with me for merely living and breathing, so much so I didn't want to be living and breathing. Sometimes Mum would try and calm Dad down, so he would turn on her instead. "See, see, you're even causing trouble between your bitch mother and me."

The stairs from the 1st floor to the top floor curved upward and the carpet was always worn and torn. I cursed these stairs whenever they became my escape route from my father. How many times did I accumulate bumps falling down those fucking stairs? And Dad would always add a few more.

These things made me scared of my father, but he wasn't always mean. He tried to teach us how to make rotis – round Indian breads. He pinched off two small pieces of dough and handed them to Sheila and me. He showed us how to flatten the dough with our palms, and then we put it on a flat pan to cook. We watched our Dad's normal shaped roti cooking with our two mini rotis, about two inches in diameter. He gave us our rotis to eat. But I was so proud of my own, I didn't eat it. I carried it around with me until it hardened and crumbled. The pride in my father's face at our childish accomplishments made me so happy. So the next time he made rotis, we rushed up for our little pieces of dough. Dad was swaying over the balls of dough with a rolling pin. The flattened rotis weren't round, but misshapen and with holes in them. "Daddy, give us our roti!" We clambered around him.

"Fuck off, leave me alone! You're going to make me burn the food." Drunkenness caused dribble to escape from the corner of his mouth. How does a confused 5-year-old think? I don't know anymore, because I'm now a confused 31 year old.

The confusing thing was that Dad was not mean all the time. He let us jam with him, using an assortment of Indian musical instruments. He loved drumming on his tabla. He drummed with his fingers on any surface he could find, even our heads. This rhythmic massage would send me to sleep. "Dadda play drums on my head, please." And he would play a song or two on my skull. He also taught me the multiplication tables and how to spell 'Czechoslovakia' by turning it into a song.

Another time, after breaking something, I ran out of the kitchen, knowing that my father would be behind me to punish me. I think it was his favourite hobby. "Dolly! Come back here, you bitch." I was at the top of the stairs, looking through the banisters. "No!" I yelled back. I saw from his expression that he couldn't be arsed to climb the stairs to get me. Suddenly the anger drained from his face like pus out of a boil. "Okay, Dolly, I'm sorry I shouted at you. Come down and give you Dada a hug. Do you forgive me?"

Of course I forgave him: I was a child and he was my Dad. I came down the stairs to give him a hug. But his were the open arms of an electric chair, because as soon as I was in arm's reach, he pulled my hair and smacked me around the face.

I began thinking about running away. I liked the idea of living on the streets – it would be an adventure. I had recently seen a documentary about Brazilian street kids living in a homemade shack, and crazily I was jealous of these kids. Maybe because there were no parents in the picture. Taking pointers from cartoons, I made a bindle out of a pillowcase and tree branch. It took me ages to tie the knotted pillowcase to the stick. I filled it up with biscuits, a couple of t-shirts and a toothbrush, and slung it over my shoulder. I went down to the front door and opened it, but I was too scared of the outside world. Dad told us it was full of devils and baddies who would kill us and eat us. Unable to go out, I went inward. I pretended the top bedroom was a strange land to explore, full of hollowed out trees that took me into magical underworlds.

Occasionally Dad took me on strange outings. I went with him to St George's Hospital to watch a doctor drain a lump on my Dad's head. Or he took me to the pub and made me wait outside. A couple of times he took me to dole office in Tooting to sign on. He didn't go to the one in Streatham because he didn't want anyone seeing him on the dole. He told everyone he met he was a successful actor and musician. When someone claimed not to know who he was, he shook his head derisively. If he had an argument with someone at The John Company, his local, he would buy a bottle of whiskey and sit on a bench on Tooting Common. He forced me to sit next to him stock-still. The psychiatric patients still used the common, enduring 10-hour mystical meditations on park benches, talking the linguistics of stars and demons. Sometimes I talked to a few. I noticed ordinary people crossing the road to avoid these people. I painfully understood this ostracism. The neighbourhood kids crossed the road when they saw us, calling us stuck-up for not playing with them. These patients on day-release told me their life stories of being Jesus, God, the Queen. It didn't matter to me there was more than one Jesus. I liked their stories. I liked all stories.

Further down Keymer Road lived an old woman who liked playing the piano, and I liked listening to her play. Miss Turner came around one day, asking if she could take Sheila and I took her local church to attend the Sunday School. My father professed to be Christian, and since he had been praying quite a lot (for a pools win), he happily let us go. Hitherfield Baptist Church was a five-minute walk away at the bottom of a hill. Miss Turner came around every Sunday to take us to church. I loved Sunday school. The teachers were the kindest people I met. Two stand out in my mind, and they were a married couple, Mr and Mrs Matthews. Mr Matthews had a beard and in my naiveté I thought he was a relative of Jesus. We played hangman, guessing bible quotes; and we sang lots of songs. I was reading greedily by now. Mum had initially taught me how to spell using alphabet cards, and whenever I came across a word, such as on a cereal packet, I annoyed my Mum by asking what it was. I began cutting words out on whatever I could lay my hands on and inventing sentences with them. I carried this with me to Sunday school, always entering contests, and usually winning, taking home prizes such as stickers with sayings on them. Some of them I stuck on my bed, some my Dad took for himself. He stuck one sticker on his armchair: 'I am the apple of God's eye' was plastered over his drunken, drooling head.

Next door to the church was Hitherfield School. I had been attending the nursery for not too long before joining the infant school. Nursery was just a haze of painted hands and sandpits. We sang songs too. Usually I got the words wrong. For example, instead of singing, "Who built the ark? Noah – Noah. Who built the ark? Brother Noah built the ark." I sang: "Who built the ark – no one – no one. Who built the ark, bloody no one built the ark!"

The other kids made fun of my name. "Dolly? Dolly is a doll. Dolly is a doll!" they teased. I found it difficult making friends. People taking turns to talk were a novel experience to me. The other kids would talk to me and I'd stand there like a naa-naa, not understanding that I had to reply. They soon got bored of me. I was reading more fluidly than I spoke. My speech development was haphazard, crude and weak. This was not surprising; the two people who taught me to speak were a slurring, swearing drunk and a deaf, speech-impeded mother. I stuttered. People laughed. So I stuttered some more, almost tearful from the embarrassment. Books and stories didn't make fun of me, didn't answer back, so I was usually in the corner with the books, or painting more pictures than words uttered.

I loved my infant school teachers. The one I remember the best is Mrs Lyons. She was kind and nurturing, really made learning a pleasure and adventure. I absorbed her praise and approval like a sponge. "That's a great story, Dolly" or "That's such a nice picture, I'm going to put it up near my desk." I loved learning. I preferred being at school to being at home. I'm laughing bitterly as I write this, you see I know what happens next...

As my Dad told me a thousand times the world was an evil place, and it was up to him to save us. The outside world stayed on the other side of our council house door. Although I didn't really understand people, I didn't think they were evil. People looked at me funnily and said cruel things but they kept their distance. But there were hundreds of beatings from my protector. I don't even remember the reasons behind half of them. I don't think my father knows either. Dad didn't realise he brought the evil to us. Dad was regularly visited by a friend; the bastard sexually abused me almost every time he visited. I was too scared to tell anyone about it. But in the end I didn't have to. I had contracted a venereal infection. The doctor told my parents I had been sexually abused too. The look of disgust and anger in my father's eyes made me want to disappear. I can't remember what he said to me after that but I wouldn't talk about it, I couldn't talk about it. The next thing I recall is being interrogated by schoolteachers about who did this to me. Did it happen at the school? I was crowded by lots of big adult faces. I said yes to all their questions just to get rid of them. I have no memory of the time directly after that, except more people looked disgusted with me, my Dad especially.

I became more withdrawn. The playground was a world full of laughter and I was in the corner watching. When I went to bed at night, I prayed not to wake the next morning. I stopped liking going to school, yet I didn't want to go home. All I wanted was my books and my daydreams. The only good memory of that time was the birth of my sister Paula. I had talked to her through the womb wall, telling her how I felt. My Mum was certain she talked back. Actually, I think I'm to blame for Paula's subsequent talkativeness. She just doesn't shut up! But I wouldn't have her any other way.

I carried my new sister around a lot, telling her stories. Being only about six myself, I did drop her a couple of times, which I was punished for. Then one day she was whisked away to Brompton Hospital. I thought it was my fault for dropping her. The doctors found a hole in her heart. So playing on wards was happening again, but this time I had Sheila and Kenny with me. There were lots of toys to play with and a rocking horse I rode around the world with. The nurses loved Kenny, and he loved the nurses. If he went missing, we usually found him in the nurse's station hugging them and giving them kisses.

Sometimes Mum stayed at the hospital, so it was up to Dad to look after the three of us. He spent most of the money he had on drinks, and when he did go out to buy food, he bought us meals we didn't like. "Daddy, I don't like bubble and squeak." He'd insult and argue with God. "Why are you punishing me by giving me these children!"

Kenny, Sheila and I shared one bed, and we ate, talked, played and slept there. I went to school in dirty clothes, and was called fleabag by the other kids. Paula did eventually recover but I began to think it was normal for siblings to be near death as babies. And I did feel deserted. Because of that, I liked being sick. I was jealous of the attention Sheila and Paula had when they were ill. If I fell over and scraped my knee, I would smile. I knew I'd get some attention that way. I even had fantasies of staying in hospital.

It was too much for my Dad. When my Mum said she wanted another baby, Dad positively jogged into the vasectomy clinic and had the snip. My Mum said she would have had 10 kids if she could. As a teenager I hated my Mum for this, for begetting small creatures for the world to abuse. I almost felt like she had babies to use as an excuse not to look after and protect the older kids. It was definitely a compulsion for her. I remember one time hearing what I thought was a baby crying in an alleyway. I told my Mum about this. She said, "Go out and see. If it is a baby, let's keep it and not tell anyone." It turned out to be a cat. My Mum was so disappointed she almost cried.

The beatings lessened but my Dad became stricter. He wouldn't let us go out as much. The only places were allowed to go was school, church and the supermarket. "I told you the world was evil, and now *you* are turning evil," he said to me. It didn't stop him going out into this evil world to get drunk and add his own evil.

When my parents argued it was hell. Hell is the impossibility of reason (or reasons for impossibility). Both parents wanted us to take sides, but their arguments were so irrational and bizarre, we kids just didn't know what the fuck to say or do. Silence

42

was preferable to talk I found. Silence never bullshits.

Whenever there was a chance to go out, I jumped at it. I loved the shopping every Thursday, well almost every Thursday, sometimes Dad spent the whole giro on booze. The contingency plan when this happened was then to dive behind sofa for small change and steal milk from people's doorsteps. Occasionally Dad had to sell something. He said he had to do it if we were going to eat. He'd be gone for hours and hours, while our stomachs churned their empty liquids out of hunger and fear. We knew Dad would come back without the pawned item *and* without the money too. We heard the door open; he was drunk of course, calling the whole world a bastard for not being able to close the front door. We didn't complain to him that we were still hungry.

Anyway, I loved the journey from the house to the shops. In my mind it was always an adventure, with ghosts and ghouls to conquer. First, there was a house near Dunraven School, the curtains drawn open. The living room walls were painted black with strange pictures. I had read an article in the local papers about the woman who lived there: she was a witch and proud of it. Initially I was scared of her. The teenagers from the local school made fun of her. I knew how that felt, and she always had a smile for me. In the end, I wanted to be her. People were afraid of her, and left her alone. She had power over them. People left me alone, but they ignored me. I had no power whatsoever. Every time I passed her window I would always peer into her window, hopeful to see some magic. Then we passed a large deserted house; to me it was a mansion. It had been gutted by fire. I don't know the story behind it. Mum told me the family that lived there died. I was convinced they were still there, peering through the blackened windows. I always ran past it as fast as I could, thinking they were chasing me for being curious. The next obstacle was the wall of a telephone exchange. I'd jump on and pretend it was a tightrope. Then I'd weave in and out some bushes. This was Leigham Avenue in Streatham, and it led to the high street and its stores, where we did our shopping.

I stuck to my Mum like glue. I guess I felt safe with her. Not that she'd protect me from Dad, but that she wouldn't hit me herself. Mum's bedtime stories were altogether different from my Dad's. She'd tell me stories about Elvis giving away his cars to total strangers. She said one woman was standing outside a car showroom, looking at a car she couldn't afford to buy. Elvis saw her and bought the car for her. I liked this story. So the next time I went shopping with my Mum, I stood outside a toyshop, waiting for Elvis to walk by!

My Mum got me a deflated space hopper for my birthday. In its inflated state, it was a big orange rubber ball with horns and a painted face. You were supposed to sit on it, hold onto its horns, and bounce along. Mum took me to the local petrol station to inflate the bugger. Going to the petrol station was a happy outing for me, a novel experience. The station attendant made silly voices as he helped to inflate the hopper. As I bounced along, I had a silly grin on my face I couldn't get rid off. I fell off a couple of times but I was happy. Especially when I passed kids on the street, who gave me envious glances. I had never been in that situation before, of having something others hadn't.

We called our grandpa on our father's side Dada. I visited him every week with my Mum. To walk to his house, we always passed Streatham Common. I liked playing chase there, with the stars. I always won. Except one time when I saw a shooting star. I didn't mind letting it win. To me Dada was always old. He certainly felt old. Whenever I visited him he'd complain about the pain he felt in his joints. Or he'd complain nobody visited him – except my Mum and me. To be truthful, I didn't want to visit him either. Listening to somebody whine and complain incessantly for an hour was not something I looked forward to as a child. But I had my good times with him too. He taught me children hymns and would laugh at my stories of my mischievous siblings.

He had a streak of paranoia and an active imagination, which my Dad and I inherited. He thought everybody was after his money. He kept it in an old wrinkled carrier bag under the mattress of his bed. His mistrust was justified when it came to my Dad. He said when Dada died he was going straight to that carrier bag before anyone else did. There were times when debt-ridden because of his drinking, that my Dad would lament my grandfather's existence.

I visited him regularly until I was in my late teens. His pain and paranoia had worsened. He falsely accused me of stealing his pots and pans, and told me not to come back. I didn't. I had been waiting for that relinquishment of duty and was relieved when it came. Although when I thought about him sitting all alone I wanted to cry. I thought everything I said and did hurt somebody somewhere. Depression smiles when these thoughts arise.

But back to school, well, it was back to school. Hitherfield Junior School was separated from Hitherfield Infants by a field. I always looked across the field to the bigger kids in envy; they looked so grown up. I couldn't wait to be there. When it was my time to go there, Dada gave me some money to get school things. My Dad took my money and spent it all on drinks. The new term was a few days away, and I had a hole in my shoe, and no pencils. So my Dad took me on a shopping trip. First stop – the bookies, where Dad grabbed a bunch of pencils emblazoned with the bookies' name. Next was Tesco in Streatham High Street. We went to the clothing section on the first floor; the supermarket was on the ground floor. Tesco, in those days, had both the left and right shoes in display boxes. He gave me the cheapest pair to try on; they fitted okay. "Now put your old shoes in the box." He ordered. "Why?" "Just do it!" I walked with him towards the checkout and paused at the tills. But

Dad didn't stop. Instead he pushed me towards the exit, and then out of the shop, pausing only to look at the cashier's tits.

If I thought going to junior's school would be a new start, I was wrong. The head teacher, Mrs Keitch, was a bitch, and of course my father told her so. She treated everyone like shit, but because she now hated my Dad, she really let me have it. She had that look of disgust that most adults cultivated. She probably had another chat with my father, so like every beautiful human being exercised her right to utilise the psychological defence mechanism of displacement upon someone smaller, weaker. She made me stand up in assembly in front of everybody, and would criticise and insult me. One occasion that stands out was when she told me to stand up in assembly and asked me why I didn't sign up for the cycle proficiency class. "I don't have a bike." I told her. I must be a comedian, because she was unable to stop laughing. "You're pathetic, Dolly," she had great fun in telling me. Most of the students and staff hated her but were too scared to stand up to her, except at the yearly school raffle when people protested that Mr Keitch always won first prize. But at least I stopped bedwetting.

In the first year of junior school, our teacher asked the class. "Could you all stand up, one at a time, and tell me your father's job." I dreaded my turn. "Dolly, stand up and tell me what your father does." At first I was going to answer, "He beats the shit out of us." But instead I said, "He's a film actor."

"Now, Dolly, it's not nice to lie. What is his real job?"

"That is his real job; he works in films."

"Sit down, Dolly!" My classmates smirked and sniggered.

It around this time that I began to work quite regularly as a film extra myself.

I had worked in films previously, but the first film I remember working on is one of the Star Wars movies 'The Empire Strikes Back' with my sister Sheila.

First we had to audition. We were told there and then we were hired and were measured up for our costumes. With our Dad as our chaperone, we worked on the film for about a week. Being an extra involves a lot of sitting around waiting to be called onto the set. Extras always look forward to meal times. Breakfast was always a tea and coffee urn, with sausage, bacon or egg in a roll. Although I'm vegetarian now, whenever I smell bacon or sausages being cooked, it always reminds me happily of those days.

There were 10 other kids with us, most from stage school. One of the production assistants realised it wasn't fair for us children just to sit around, so he let us play on the part of the set not being used. The set was a labyrinth of white space age tunnels and futuristic cloisters. I always wanted a wendy house but this was much better. The 12 of us played chase, and had shoot-em-ups with prop guns. Our scene was going to be filmed after lunch, so after we ate, we were put into our costumes. Every single one of us had to wear a pair of green trousers and a green jumper that itched like hell. We were also given a circuit board each, which were to be our schoolbooks.

Finally called on to the set, we had to walk down a gangway with a teacher. A silver C3PO also shared our scene. Again we had to wait around between shooting. Sheila and I used this time to explore the set. We saw Chewie, which made Sheila cry. The guy inside had to take off the furry head to reassure her. All sorts of ghouls and monsters walked about. The longer I was there, the less I believed it was make-believe. I carried the feeling with me that it was a documentary. I liked this world, more interesting than ordinary life. Empire Strikes Back is basically about the battle between the forces of good and evil, and I felt part of it.

I saw our journey from our home to the studio as a space ship ride taking me to another world. "Where you going?" Fred the window cleaner asked us. "I'm going into outer space." I told him proudly. Planet Earth was purely a stepping-stone.

I didn't like planet Earth – it had my Dad and school on it.

Every spring during junior school we were all given a daffodil bulb, the one that flowered the best won a prize. And every year while the others flowered and shone in the sunlight, mine just looked like a fucking onion. The first year I didn't even water it. Nobody told me you had to. I began to think they didn't want to explain things to me because they needed someone to laugh at or look down to. And boy did they laugh. I invited my classmates one year to my birthday party. "Yeah, we'll come," almost everyone said. This made me very happy. On the day of my birthday party I waited by the door for the people to come, with an excited smile. But I waited. And waited. And waited. Nobody turned up. They thought it was a great joke to play on me. I was learning that the world is full of laughter.

I stopped bothering with people after that. I wrote stories, I drew, and I threw myself into my schoolwork. Academically I sailed past my peers; I was miles ahead. I read compulsively. There literally weren't enough books in the school for me to read. There was talk about moving me up a year, yet there were concerns I wouldn't make friends there. Not that I had friends in the year I already was in. In the end it didn't happen, I don't know why. After every lunch I sat alone in the field making a thousand feet of childhood daisy chains. Playtime – everyone couldn't wait for it but I hated it. To be alone and silent in the midst of screams, laughter and games. I have this picture of me standing alone in a playground for the thousand days that was my childhood.

But at least at school I wouldn't go hungry. I loved school dinners. I found it hard to concentrate on my work as lunchtime approached and the foody aromas drifted from the kitchen to the classrooms. I almost drooled at the thought of soft fish fingers and mouth-melting caramel tart. Sometimes at home the only food we had was a slice of bread covered in a meat paste or cornflakes. There was one school outing to the coast when we were told to bring a packed lunch. My Mum and Dad had been arguing violently so I didn't bring the subject up, and there wasn't much food anyway. On the coach ride there I went into people's bags to steal food. One girl caught me and she protested very loudly. I tried to laugh her off but inside I was crying with shame.

Because the family had no money I hated sponsorship-based fundraising. I was always guaranteed to bring in the least money, if anything at all. There was only my Mum and Dad to get money from and they never had any. Parents evening was always fun. If it was a female teacher, my Dad spoke directly to her tits. After one teacher told my father my work was in decline, Dad told the teacher he had permission to beat the shit out of me the next time I was out of line. Oh shit, I thought, it's happening again. The faces. Why do humans have faces? I watched my teacher's expression change from indifference to disgusted pity.

A few times Dad collected us from school. He would play the fool for my classmates. "Your Dad is so funny." One said.

"Yes, hilarious." I said, remembering the soul-destroying insults he gave me when I didn't laugh at his jokes. He only acted the caring father if people were watching. Why can't you be like that without an audience? I wanted to ask him.

But usually Mum would collect us from school. We were able to tell from her expression if Dad was drunk or not. The school was at the bottom of a steep hill. Every day, after school, we had to climb that hill. Sometimes I pretended I was climbing Mount Everest to make it more fun. At the top of the hill, if we wanted to visit the sweetshop we had to turn right through a wide alleyway behind the John Company pub. The newsagent always had a harassed look on his face. No bloody wonder, with 50 kids charging up to the counter, while another 5 shoplifted. If I ever had a little bit of change I usually picked the same sweets: pink prawns, bubble gum, sugar dummies, and candy bracelets.

If our Dad was drunk, we had to sneak quietly into the house. Typically he was asleep in the living room. So we had to tiptoe around him, and watch the TV with the volume off. One time I had the misfortune of having hiccups whilst Dad was sleeping his usual 15 hours a day. "Shut the fuck up! I'm trying to sleep!" I held my breath, I went to the other side of the house, I drank glasses of water, but my hiccups came back even louder. "That's it!" he snapped as whipped out of bed. He grabbed my lips. "SHUT...THE...FUCK...UP!"

"Hic!"

Punch after punch after punch into a child's body.

He stopped my hiccups.

When Dad wasn't in, the house was full of laughter and excited screams. Then the front door opened and slammed shut. Instant silence. Instant death of childhood.

A typical interaction between me and my Dad:

"Dolly!"

"Yeah," I replied meekly.

"Get the thingy for the thingy."

"What?"

"You heard me!"

I left the room, my eyes popping in fear, my palm aching in mild terror. What the hell was I supposed to do? I hid in a corner waiting for the beating or the insults or the screams.

What Mrs Keitch said about not having a bike stung. After I outgrew my tricycle, I asked for a two-wheeler. "You'll get one when you're good," Dad promised. Birthdays and Christmases came and went – no bike year upon year upon year. All I wanted was a bike. Seeing other kids riding their own bikes engendered tears of jealousy. Just imagine being promised something you really want 1001 times, and not getting it 1001 times. Soon I stopped wanting … anything.

That's not strictly true. I wanted my Dad to stop beating the people I loved. What is worse than hearing the people you love screaming in pain? Mum got the brunt of it. Dad accused her of seeing other men, which was bullshit. She never, ever left the house alone. When my Mum was pregnant for the 5th time and Dad found out, I really doubted we would all see the day out alive. "You fucking prostitute! Whose baby is it?" Dad screamed at Mum. "It's yours, it's yours!" "Don't fucking lie! I had a vasectomy!" Furniture went flying over our heads. "Please don't hurt Mummy!" we begged our Dad. We were kicked aside. "You fat whore." He said to his pregnant wife every day for 9 months.

By the time Sammy was born, there was no doubt he was my Dad's; they had the same eyes and nose. There is a period of time after a vasectomy when you shouldn't have unprotected sex, and of course my father didn't pay attention to this.

Where did our names come from? Dad named us all after grandparents, drinking buddies and women he wished he shagged. At Sammy's christening, I was too ill to attend. Instead of postponing the service, Dad left me at home alone. Mum volunteered to stay and look after me. "We need two parents, stupid," he told my Mum. Once again, the TV set was my babysitter. On it was an extra-terrestrial with a triangular head and beady eyes entering somebody's house. I thought the alien was going to visit our house next. I turned off the TV and hid behind the sofa, sobbing quietly.

You could say by now I was beginning to hate my father. Children will take a lot of shit from their parents before something changes forever in that child. I kept out his way, and stayed with Mum all the time. As Dad's drinking worsened, he was less and less able to deal with running the household. Because Mum was deaf, I became her ears and voice. It was up to me to make the phone calls and interpret for her when she went out. My mother was not worldly-wise and she made me ask silly, naïve questions. If I refused to ask the question, she would get tearful and say, 'It's not my fault I'm deaf.' My mother never laid a hand on me but she was the queen of emotional blackmail. One instance I recall is when I had to phone a TV repair shop because our TV went bust. I interpreted for my

Mum word for word. The conversation went something like this:

"Our TV's not working."

"What kind is it?"

"The colour kind."

"No, what make is it?"

"It is an electrical one."

(sniggers) "What's wrong with it?"

"The light doesn't come on."

"Where is it exactly?"

"It's round the back."

By this time, the TV repairman was wetting himself. "We got a right one here!" he told his colleagues.

His response skinned me alive. Can you understand why catatonia is a valid lifestyle choice?

Looking back now, I am dismayed how much responsibility was heaped on my young shoulders. Sometimes I resisted the role thrust on me. I wanted to be a child. After all, I was one. My Dad's favourite comeback was: "In India, children go to work at 5 years old. You're just lazy." He'd say, sitting slumped in an armchair, drinking, farting and swearing.

Part of my story-telling bent came from telling Mum in a condensed version what was being said on TV. This was in the days before teletext. If the stories were boring, I'd make up my own. This sometimes caused problems. Mum would ask, "What happened to that guy with the beard?" "Oh, he drowned at sea." 5 minutes later the guy with the beard turned up. "I thought you said he was dead." "Oh my God – he's a ghost!"

As if they didn't already have enough to pick on me for, some kids at school made fun of my Mum's disability. "Your Mum is deaf and dumb, dumb like you." I punched and kicked the little motherfuckers. And they were little. I was growing phenomenally. Height-wise, I was a head taller than most of my peers, and by the time I was ten I had size 34 tits and periods from hell.

Mum tried her best to liven things up for us. Lambeth Social Services used to host a yearly Deaf Xmas Party and Mum would take us along. The earlier parties had 100s of guests, a dance troupe, celebrity guests (if you can call Patrick Moore a celebrity), and expensive prizes. But with every passing year, there was less and less funding available for these functions, and the parties got smaller and smaller. The last year of these parties only 12 people turned up (6 of which were just my family) and first prize for a contest was a can of cola.

At one of these parties, a social worker unwisely gave my Dad the Santa costume to wear to hand out presents. They weren't really presents but a black bag full of satsumas. When it was time for Dad to come on stage, he was too drunk to walk in a straight line. He wasn't wearing his Santa hat and his white beard was on sideways. He walked into a table and slurred, "You stupid cunt!" which scared some kids off. "Hang on a minute," some kid said, "Santa Claus ain't Indian!" "Come here, you little shit!" my Dad slurred at him. He gave the kids who pushed to the front all of the satsumas, and the little kids at the back got nothing. There were a lot of upset kiddies that year...

Each of these parties was memorable less for its own content and more for the journeys there and back. One year the Brixton riots broke out and we were right in the middle of it; the bus we were on had to take a detour. Another year we partook in that great Asian tradition of squeezing as many people into the Mini of an Indian deaf man and his family – 12 was our record.

Ordinarily a typical Christmas for us was as follows: "Merry Christmas," I'd cheer. "Merry Christmas!" my siblings chorused. "You're all a bunch of fucking cunts!" Dad would respond.

I have a few good memories of my time at Hitherfield Junior School. The school had a bowling green, but I never saw a single person bowl on it in all my time there. It was decided a pond would be built there. I volunteered to help with a few other kids. The teacher overseeing the project was a bit of an archaeology nut so he asked us as we dug to keep an eye of for anything unusual. In the end we found bits of broken crockery and farm animal bones. Behind the trees in the bowling green there was the ruins of a pigsty. We did some research and found out the school was built on farmland. I loved that the earth had bits of history in it, and I loved watching the pond take shape and the tadpoles turn into frogs.

During one of my father's sober periods where he had aspirations to be a normal human being, he signed the consent form for my year's school journey. This usually was a 5-day stay in the countryside. My year was going to Marchant's Hill, in Surrey. On the morning, the coach was going to pick us up from the school, my Dad blocked the front door, refusing to let me leave. "Please don't go," he sobbed. "Somebody's going to hurt you. I know it. Please don't go."

"But I want to go."

My Mum pulled my Dad away from the door and opened it. "I'll be okay, Daddy." I kissed him and left for the school with my Mum.

At the school lots of kids were crying as they were separated from their parents. Not me. I bounced happily onto the coach and waved goodbye to my Mum.

At Marchant's Hill, there were lots and lots of wooden huts, which housed the dormitories of the many schools staying there. Marchant's Hill started life in the war as a camp for evacuees, we were told. There were schools from all over the country there, it was the English version of summer camp. Because we were from London, and the only one with people of colour, the other schools were scared of us. I liked this feeling.

I had a good time there. My favourite thing was going for a 6-mile hike in the woods with my school. In my mind I was alone in the wilderness, living off the land. I have no idea what the other kids did to this day. I had a veruca and newly discovered lice on my head, so everyone gave me a wide berth – more than usual, that is. At the end of our stay there was a disco. When the music stopped, so we have to, somewhat like musical chairs. I won, so I was flushed with happiness and smiling at everyone, nobody was smiling back at me. Somebody pulled me aside and said, "You can't dance; you're crap." I kept out of everybody's way after that and went off by myself climbing trees and drawing schematics for a tree house I was going to build as a hideaway from the world. My Dad was right – somebody was going to hurt me.

But my best memory of that period was my time in the 5 a side girls football team. We were coached by Mr Vanstone to enter a London tournament. In actuality he concentrated primarily on the boys' team, and the girls' team was an afterthought. The boys were kicked out in the first few rounds but we girls won our first few matches comprehensively. To be candid, the team was one girl – Dorritt. She was a tomboy who played football with the boys every break time. The rest of the team had their moments of glory, though. There was one game we were on the verge of losing 2-0.

Five minutes from time, I scored unexpectedly. And unexpectedly the rest of the team came to hug me or slap my back. I only had a few moments like that in my childhood. In the last minute of the game we equalised. It was all down to penalties now.

Deborah was in goal. I could hardly bear to look. But she was brilliant: she saved more goals than what went in, and we were the South London winners for our age group. We hugged and congratulated her. We were all positively glowing.

We were awarded a silver medal by a senior police officer, and our picture appeared in the local paper. I should have known better than to tell my Dad of our victory. "Who the fuck cares? You should get a medal for being so fat and ugly." At the time that hurt, but I realised later how pathetic my father was for being jealous of his own daughter.

In my last year at Hitherfield, the council moved us to a bigger place – a four bed roomed flat on Streatham Hill. The flat was part of a Victorian house. The rooms were huge and the ceilings high. Poor little Sammy kept getting lost in the flat. A few of the rooms had a bell built into the wall; its original purpose was to call the maid to that room. The living room window overlooked the main road of Streatham Hill and directly opposite was Streatham Hill Theatre, then used primarily as a bingo hall, but occasional theatrical show would play there, one of which I saw at a school outing. Famous plays, famous faces and royalty saw the inside of its walls. When we first moved there, theatrical costumes were still being kept behind one of its windows, and I was convinced there was a ghost there that liked to wear these costumes. I told this to my siblings, and we were too scared to look out of the window for days after that. When I wanted to sleep while my siblings were being rowdy, all I had to do was tell them the bingo hall ghost was in the doorway. They would dive under the covers and keep quiet after that! I was learning from my Dad.

Now in 2002 the shops on Streatham Hill are the same you find in any cosmopolitan district, full of fast food stores, ethnic restaurants, mini cab offices and off licences. It very different when we moved to Streatham Hill in October 1980. The shops were as posh as hell: a fur shop, a wig shop, haberdashers and a piano shop. I felt too intimidated to go into them, and they always gave my Mum and us five boisterous kids condescending looks. I have no doubt if we were American we'd be trailer trash.

It was also around this time we went on our first holiday as a family. We had gone on days out to seaside resorts, not that we have any mementos of those days. When the photos came back from the developers, there weren't many pics of us kids in it. This was because my father aimed the camera mostly at women in bikinis.

In 1981 the 7 of us went to Blackpool, and we had quite a good time. The weather was fair and Dad stayed relatively sober. The next year we went back again and my father stayed pissed throughout the whole holiday. He picked a fight with everyone he met. You could see he was just itching for someone to bump into him, so he could lay into them. His day was not complete if he did not do this. The one incident that stands out in my mind was when we all in an amusement arcade. We weren't allowed to play, we were forced to watch Dad get angrier and angrier at a fruit machine bearing bruised fruit, his swearing getting louder and louder. "You fucking cunt!" He kicked and shook the machine, everyone in the arcade looking at us. "What am I praying to you God for? You never listen to me!" he screamed.

One of the arcade workers told my father, quite nicely, not to shake the machine. My Dad grabbed the man and slurred, "You're being mean to me because you're racist, aren't you?"

The poor guy looked nonplussed.

"Daddy, stop it." We chorused.

"Fucking shut up! You kids always embarrassed me. Look, look, at how everybody is looking at us. You always shame me up!"

Our Dad didn't come to subsequent holidays with us to Blackpool.

In September 1982 I moved to secondary school, St Martins in Tulse Hill, South London. I don't have many clear memories of my secondary school. That's not surprising – I think all they taught me was that suicide was a nicer alterative. No inspiring teachers, no interesting subjects, the only people spending more time on me than the usual fleeting few seconds were the bullies – pupils and teachers both.

Even though I was quite sporty in Hitherfield, I hated P.E. at St Martins. We had to wear this brown mini skirt; I hated it. I didn't like showing my legs – because only perverts and bruises came near my legs. Dad introduced yet another paedophile to the family and that motherfucker had his fun with me.

Anyway, Miss O'flynn was our P.E. teacher and taught me nothing but the fact she was possibly angrier than my father. Ah, man, the screaming fits she had. Why was the world always screaming? It makes you wonder if some people become teachers for the power trip. It's pathetic they only way you can exercise power in your life is through demeaning children. There were few teachers at that school that weren't fucked up. There was an alcoholic music teacher who made us sing, 'Suicide is Painless'. How about the anorexic English teacher who would weigh herself in the nurse's office between every lesson. There was another English teacher, Mr Ayres, I think he was called. He was a bit of a hippy. We only read two books and wrote a few essays under his yearlong tutelage. Instead he wanted us to get in touch with ourselves, or damn shit like that. He wanted us to share our stories, but we only heard the loudest, and their stories were never interesting. My only friend at the school was Judith, a Black girl who came from Brixton. I think we learned more about books from each other than our English teachers. We also wrote stories for each other.

There were two girls in my class who made my life hell – Angela and Michelle. They always made fun of the way I talked, walked, my cheap clothes. At one of my worst incidents at school, they were the ones that laughed the loudest. Taking off my shorts that I wore under my P.E. skirt, I pulled off my threadbare knickers. "Ergh," Michelle jeered. "Look at Dolly's knickers, look at the holes in them. Yuk!" Laughter. Laughter. Laughter. And I stood there in the middle of it. Another similar incident happened soon after. I couldn't change from my P.E. t-shirt into my blouse quick enough and someone saw I was wearing a bra that was obviously too small. Clothes were at the bottom of the household shopping list, right below important things like alcohol and cigarettes. My classmates looked at me with looks of disgust and pity, or whales of laughter. I shrank away from my skin but my heart was still beating. The fucker was still beating. One girl took me aside and told me nicely that I needed a bigger bra. The whole incident was upsetting, but her kind word both helped and hurt me. I already knew I needed a bigger bra. I had tried to bring it up with my parents. "Why are you growing big tits like a tart?" Dad said.

I had to see an orthodontist at this time, who said I needed to wear a brace because my bottom teeth jutted out and I looked like a monkey. Adults say the nicest things.

The only good times during that period was working as extras in films. At the studios I liked exploring the sets, the fake building fronts. Behind the doors there was nothing. Reality was turning into a movie set – there was nothing behind it.

Indiana Jones and the Temple of Doom was being filmed in England under the direction of Steven Spielburg. They needed about 50 Indian kids to be child slaves in a mine, so myself, Sheila and Kenny went along. It meant some weeks of school, which was great. The school protested at first, but when the film company promised to provide teachers, they reluctantly let me go.

A coach pulled up each day from various points in London to take us up to Elstree Studios in

Hertfordshire. I think every one of us kids were overawed when we entered the studio for the first time: it was a re-creation of an underground mine – brown-rocked, rugged, dusty. I picked up a loose rock, expecting it to weigh a ton. It didn't; it was a painted polystyrene chunk. I chucked one on my brother's head. From the look in his eyes, he was ready to die. The rock merely bounced off his head – it cracked me up. Our costumes were torn, dirty grey rags. The boys had to wear turbans. Guess who was in charge of doing the turbans? Dad.

He had told the production team he was a turban specialist. This was not obvious from his first attempts. The first boy had his turban wrapped so tight he was given an instant facelift and almost fainted. The second boy's turban didn't even stay on. The pssst of a larger can opening accompanied my father's work. It was a disaster. They had to find someone else to do the turbans until my father became more adept at it.

After putting on our rags, we were sprayed with liquid dirt – we looked like slaves all right. A production assistant, who was bit of a bastard really, looked after us. He teased this overweight boy about his tits. "You're supposed to be an undernourished slave not a tub of lard with tits! No desserts for you!" The first week he attempted to control as like a sergeant major, barking orders. He soon tired of that, and spent the rest of the time trying to get into the knickers of any adult female working on the lot.

The first scene shot with the kids, we had to cross a plank over a flaming gorge recreated in a studio.

The gorge was quite deep and burning with sinister fires; it was actually quite scary. The first few shots, I was too frightened to cross the plank, but it was easy to sink into make-believe. I imagined my father chasing me with a whip and so I ran along the plank over the flames. What a rush that was! I repeated the act again and again. I like this world better than the world outside.

During the next few weeks we broke a lot of rocks and were whipped a lot – great fun! One scene involved us being whipped by a guard as we carried our rocks. My Dad was one of the guards. He became the role, whipping each child that passed him with his fake whip. Another guard near him whipped Kenny across the arse, forcing him to jump in the air. Our Dad saw this and threatened to kill his fellow extra. "Don't you fucking hurt my son!" Of course, that was *his* job.

I think we were working for about three weeks when I first saw Steven Spielberg. He came to direct a scene with us kids in it. About half way through the day, he began to look directly at me. I was embarrassed but flattered too. I hoped he was going to give me a bigger part. At the end of the day I was told by one of the chaperones I was no longer needed.

"Why?" I asked, almost crying.

"Don't take this personally, but you're too adult-like to be a child slave. I know you're only 12, but you have the body of a woman. You're not needed any more, I'm sorry."

Yes, I was 5ft 7in, with a 36 bust. A body of a woman, maybe. Didn't stop me crying like a child, though. Thanks Mr Spielberg. I guess my and the fat boy's tits were just too big for you.

Because people were laughing *at* him a lot, Dad thought he was a great comedian. He practiced his jokes on his children, and we laughed because we didn't want to get insulted. Whenever we were working on a film or TV programme, he would act the comedian in front of the director or producer. They were not impressed and just looked embarrassed. Dad was superficially charming. But stick around and watch that charm turn into hate and disgust, and believe me, you don't have to wait long. Once we got home, Dad laid into me with as much force and hell as a plane hitting the WTC. "They didn't laugh because you were with me. Look at your face, why are you looking so depressed!" Every blow alienated me from the rest of the world. I mean, where were they? They were applauding the show, I felt, laughing at me. It wasn't just me; my brothers and sister were beaten too. Dad hated the whole world, including me and my brothers and sisters, especially me and my brothers and sisters. What was it about us that brought out so much hatred and anger in him? How could I have a benevolent perception of the world, when one of the people supposed to care and nurture me, do little short of torture me? And it always seemed to me the world was also culpable of this insular genocide. I couldn't grow a daffodil in junior school but I had no problem nurturing an incipient psychosis. I would rub my skin raw until it bleed and turn up at the school nurse's office until she got bored of me. Some days I didn't speak, catatonia indulged because I had no longer anything more to say to the world. Paranoia's lessons I absorbed; I was a genius at it. Nobody told me I was a mind reader. Everybody's mind was a boring read, except the ones that dictated my death.

Brace in a mouth that didn't know how to or want to talk.
Shoes from Tesco.
A bra that didn't fit.
Knickers that had holes in them.
A body bruised.
A body touched by dirty old man
And ignored by the rest of the world.

I was beginning to lose my mind...

PART TWO
It's a mad world

"To goodness and wisdom we make only promises; pain we obey." Marcel Proust.

We had badgered our parents for a dog for months but my Dad always said no. The pet shop across the road was selling mongrel pups for £10 each. We begged our Dad; he still said no. "It'd be a good guard dog. No burglars would dare to come into our flat." I offered.

My Dad had taken to nailing a board over the letterbox and some windows, convinced someone was going to firebomb our home. I don't know if the threat was real or imaginary, nevertheless he did make it his life's work to piss off everyone he met so we were pretty scared too.

So he relented and we bought a small black and brown male pup. He was so tiny and beautiful I couldn't stop hugging him. My father named him Bobby. I taught him to sit, stay and give his paw. My mother loved him because he sensed her deafness, and would modify his behaviour accordingly. If there were a doorbell or phone ringing, he'd nudge my Mum with his nose and walk her to the front door or phone. Nobody trained him to do this. I think animals have a lot more intelligence and intuition than those supposedly in the know attributes to them. Just because an animal can't talk bullshit, it is not a superior being (!) Sometimes he would answer the phone by picking up the receiver and barking down it; I tried that a few times too. And I don't believe for a minute that animals don't have a sense of humour. Nobody can tell me my dog isn't laughing at me after it has nudged me in the bum to knock me over!

Bobby loved his blanket; he carried it everywhere and sucked on it like a dummy. He liked us to put him in the centre of the blanket and then toss him in the air. He only lived to be 4 unfortunately. He swallowed part of a red sponge ball and it got stuck in his intestine. The RSPCA removed it but he was too far-gone; he didn't make it. I was heartbroken. He was the first being I loved unconditionally and he gave me back the love unconditionally. When I cried, he licked off my tears. When I needed to hug somebody, he would let me without pushing me away, and that meant so much to me. I told Kenny once that the dogs taught me how to love, and if we were going to bring children into this world, we needed that. My brother nodded but added, "But we might pat our kids on the head and feed them dog biscuits."

Bobby protected us when our Dad was effing and blindingly drunk by putting himself between our Dad and us. He took all the kicks and punches from my father but he refused to budge. And some wonder why many people prefer animals to humans.

We were all in the kitchen trying to stop our Dad hitting our Mum. Dad was about to punch Mum and Bobby bit him in the bollocks. Dad was going to bring down a chair on Bobby's head as punishment, so I grabbed my father and pushed him away. Dad stormed out and threatened to kill anyone who left the kitchen. Most of us were shaking with fear. I saw Sheila lips trembling and tears streaming down her face, so I hugged her. Paula went out onto the balcony and called out our neighbour's name and they phoned the police. Dad had taken to setting things on fire, so we would – as he hoped – be burned to death in our sleep. While we were locked in the kitchen, we heard our father stomp throughout the flat, breaking furniture, and threatening to burn down the flat. After what seemed like forever, the police came. They didn't even bother to check to see if we were okay. They spoke to my father for few minutes and just left. I was beginning to hate the whole fucking world. They didn't care. My Dad told his brother about me pushing my father away. My uncle said, "You mustn't hit your father. You have to respect your parents." I'm sorry, but I didn't know there was etiquette to brutality.

I was getting physically and psychologically weaker. I had no energy to do anything. I was barely able to stand. Tests were done and glandular fever was diagnosed. It meant a long time off school, and once I got better I just couldn't go back, I refused to go back. Then my physical health went downhill again. This time an under-active thyroid was to blame. I learnt later that not having enough of the thyroid hormone can trigger psychosis in people. Not that any doctor told me that. They didn't tell me anything, except pull you socks up and go back to school.

The first auditory hallucination I recall happened around about this time; I was 14.

Every Sunday the radio would play the UK top 40. I listened to it and taped the songs I liked. All of a sudden the music went quiet and a troll-like voice issued from the radio: "What do you want, Dolly? How much do you want?" My skin prickled. I shut of the radio in fear. Deep demonic laughter followed. "Can't get rid of me. I'm yours for life now."

"Who are you?"

"I am the universe. I choose whether you live or breathe." I got up and ran out of the room. I stopped listening to the radio from then on. As the days passed, I thought maybe I just dreamed it all. The voices then chose the TV as their medium. I was drowning in a sea of bad ads that I had to read into for cosmic significance. Soon I stopped watching TV. I became obsessed with the battle between good and evil played out in The Empire Strikes Back. I was thinking: Everybody thinks it is just a film, entertaining make-believe, but that was what *they* wanted you to think. But *that* was the reality, and the audience watching and their little lives was the fantasy.

Stress increased the hallucinations and delusions. One time Dad pressed my hand down on the oven hob; the skin of my hand sizzled and throbbed. Holding my burning hand, I ran into my bedroom. I had a picture of Jesus on the wall. I looked up at it and begged him to help me. He just stared blankly down at me, his bleeding palms facing me. Our hands looked similar. I understood then I was being persecuted for being Jesus by the demon that was my father. He wanted me to die. He was behind the voices that told me to jump down a stairwell. When I was on the street, they told me to step into oncoming traffic.

I kept myself to myself in my bedroom, just waiting for the voices to taunt me half to death again, waiting for the aliens to invade. I thought the Nazis were going to take over too. So I bought an airgun and used tin cans for practice. I became quite a good shot. I used smaller and smaller targets until I was able to knock over 2 inch toy soldiers from ten metres away. I bought a compass and taught myself map-reading using a London A-Z! I read all the books on warfare and survival I could find. I turned the space under my bed as a bunker, waiting for an ambush. I went on recon every time I left the house, looking for good places to put a sniper's nest. Or I'd stare out the window, taking down car number plates of those who I thought were spies. In all, this lasted for a year. I wrote a 300 page training manual and logistics handbook, along with 'evidence' that the invasion was taking over.

Social services became involved because I wasn't attending school. I was obviously just another case to them; they didn't really give a shit. They asked if I was having problems at home, with my Dad sitting right next to me. Social workers only offered me more humiliation and brutalisation. Every time I saw a social worker, they had that look on their face saying, 'What now?' My body was a room, where my being was huddled in a corner. Social workers did nothing to draw me out; they only made me withdraw further. I'm wondering now: did I ever hear a compassionate, useful thing from them? Because all I can remember is 'Go to school or we'll take you away from your family'. My teenage years was a place I learned there is no God, and life is as precious as your loneliness.

Looking back I can see the psychosis and social phobia wasn't addressed or treated. Not that I knew that's what I had at the time, so couldn't exactly go to someone and say, 'I have psychotic symptoms and social phobia, please help me.' Remember I was a child surrounded by adults that tut-tutted me and threatened to punish me for being sick. I wasn't physically well either. I never really recovered from the glandular fever, and I had an under active thyroid gland, which was treated inadequately. I was prescribed thyroxine to treat it, but my parents weren't up to dispensing my daily dosage. In effect, I was left in charge of my medication. Some days I took it, other days I couldn't be bothered.

The social phobia came about I think after the acerbic accumulation of too many incidents: being told off in assembly by Mrs Keitch and laughed at for not having a bike, the underwear occurrence at PE; the sexual abuse; my Dad always insulting me in public... need I go on?

This did affect how I saw the world. Across the road from our home was a Chinese takeaway. I loved Chinese food, but it took me years to pluck up the courage to go into there. I heard from one person you ordered by number, another said you ordered by name. This conflicting information made me too scared to ask, just in case I got it wrong, just in case I made a fool of myself *yet* again.

I did see a child psychiatrist at King's College. I don't remember too much about it, except the psychiatrist looked more depressed than me! I don't know to this day what was my diagnosis, if any. But after that I was no longer pestered to go back to school.

But before that happened, social services tried putting me back a year at St Martins. They thought if they put me in my sister Sheila's class, her presence would help me. I must say I thought it was a good idea too. I had high hopes.

Those high hopes were instantly deflated when I sat with my sister in assembly. Someone in my old class spotted me, and every head in that class turned to look at me, and I sat there while 30 puzzled people glared at me.

The first few days I hung out with my sister, but it was obvious her friends didn't want me around and made me feel unwelcome. There are a few other incidents I recall that happened that week. A teacher put me in charge of distributing diaries. Three girls wanted to help themselves to as many books as they liked but I said no. They laughed me off and called me a retard for being put back a year. That stung. The illness had robbed me of my intellectual functioning. I went from being near the top of my class the year previously to being unable to add up a column of numbers.

In a maths lesson later on the same day I heard disembodied voices calling me a retard. This induced a flood of tears in me. The teacher didn't know what the fuck to do. The girl I sat next to tried to comfort me but I was inconsolable. I went home that day to hear the following from my Dad: "You fucking bitch, Dolly. You always embarrass me. I've got a fucking retard, a fucking loon as a daughter. Looking at your face makes me sick."

The only peace I was getting was dreaming of death or remembering that childhood dream of the fields of gold. That night I swallowed the contents of my thyroxine medication. No death, I'm afraid. Just a heart that made its presence known by heavy palpitations and yet more life.

I needed someone to talk to – not an overworked psychiatrist or social worker, not my parents. Someone who'd understand. I hope suicide would provide a sanctuary. But I came back to life with my Dad was more pissed than a public urinal. "Why did I have you," he spat at me. "You've been nothing but shit. Someone should put you out of your misery." I agreed with him there. Since no one would do that for me, I decided to do it myself, my second suicide attempt in as many days. I locked myself in the toilet with my Dad's air gun, aiming the nozzle at my head and waiting, waiting to pull the trigger. But I couldn't do it. I was too cowardly to take the coward's way out. As I left for school that day, voices taunted me. "You can't do anything right. Life thinks you're a joke, and to death you're an even bigger joke." And they laughed at me. I was stuck in a world full of laughter. I was an exhibit in a cosmic freak show, God charging admission. Every person passing me pointed and stared and laughed, laughed, laughed. I couldn't face the derogatory voices that were connected to the humans at the school as well, so I started to bunk off.

At first I hung out at St Leonard's Church's graveyard in Streatham, amongst the crumbling headstones, talking to the dead souls, and sometimes getting a reply. Some of the graves were a few centuries old. Nobody else visited them. The graveyard was used only by alcoholics and drug addicts, and people taking a short cut. But the people in ground were my friends. Mary Ann West, for example, fell off a cliff. I asked her: did she fall, jump, or was she pushed? For some reason she was taciturn. I went to the library to find out more about the people buried in St Leonard's Church's shadow. I liked the story of the tearful mourners at the ale maker Thomas Wakenan's funeral. "What did he do with the bloody recipe?" I can imagine one of them saying. The graveyard became my second home. Dead people don't judge, dead people will stay silent – until psychosis reared its ugly head, that is.

Bored with that, I bought a travel card and just rode the buses, the underground and trains around London for a few weeks before my parents found out. I still refused to go back to school. After seeing the child psychiatrist at King's College, social services stopped bothering me. But my old man was livid that I wandered around the capital by myself. "I'm gonna lock you up until you die, you cunt!" My

Dad's inability to carry anything through meant when my Mum opened the door the next day, he decided he'd rather watch TV than protest. I was glad; it was no fun being locked in a room and having to pee into a jar.

I spent the next year sitting in an apathetic armchair, watching both my psychosis and the TV. The TV was more evil. I was too depressed to do anything else. I only had the energy to throw furniture about, break mirrors, and hate the whole world. I was turning into my father. I still felt like dying, still felt like wiping out the whole fucking world. This is probably why I thought about suicide every day. When I woke up in the morning, I said, "Fuck you, rising sun – I'd rather see death." Everything people did around me was torture, even if they were just sitting there quietly. I had a permanent black mood, and my family stayed clear of me, which just made me even more paranoid. I thought I hurt people just by living and breathing. I thought the devil was the only one paying me attention, the only one who cared what I was doing.

There were periods of catatonia. I wouldn't – or couldn't - talk for days on end. I only went out to help my Mum with shopping or to go to the library. When I tell people now I left school at 14 and didn't go back, their usual reaction is, "But you're so bright." Well, actually, I practically lived at the library. The number of books allowed out was 15, but even that wasn't enough for me. I wanted to educate myself, I decided, the state just brainwashes you. I listened to the stories of the library's resident loners of why they became loners. I made a deal with myself to read every book in the library. I found mainstream literature a bore, except for the biographies. Books about or by ordinary people I loved and connected with. They became my friends. I read one book about child abuse deaths. I spoke to these children, saying, "May you have peace, may you have fun where you are, with all the toys and animals that you want. May you smile and not get beaten up for doing it." Then I would visualise hugging that child, saying, "*I* care for you." The violence was horrendous, yes. But that isn't what causes the most pain. It's the caustic alienation. That total aloneness, where you know you can get beaten to death and not one person would save you or even acknowledge you. You die alone. You die unloved. You die rejected by the world more interested in their TV and alcohol.

There was the occasional work as a film extra, or I would go with my Dad to one of his jobs. I remember once he had to do a voice-over for the BBC, dubbing the interpreted English over an Asian voice. Of course, he needed to be soused to the gills before he had the courage to do it. He started the interpreted text smoothly – if in a somewhat slurred fashion. Halfway through he got bored and punctuated the text with swearwords and interjections like, "Who gives a fuck what this bastard thinks? Why doesn't anybody ask me *my* opinion?" Then he wondered why his agent was giving him less and less work.

One film the whole family worked on was 'Foreign Body'. No one's even heard of the bloody film. Our agent called and said a family of poor Indians were needed. So the seven of us went, including my Mum who is a red-haired, green-eyed Scot. Rather than changing into our rags once we reached location, our father made us wear our ragged clothes for the journey there and we had to travel by public transport. I was already called fleabag for wearing my normal clothes, so you can imagine what I felt like what I felt having to wear clothes Oxfam would have rejected, in public.

The worst to have it was Kenny. He was forced to wear tea-stained pink flares. Of course people pointed and laughed at him. Oh, the comedy of being a human being. Poor Kenny hasn't been the same since. He's a big strapping man now with macho pursuits, but he still screams like a woman.

There was the occasional outing the family took. We couldn't afford to go to the zoo, so we went to Battersea Dog's Home. Instead of beautiful exotic creatures to gaze upon, we had lonely, unwanted strays to look at. I was learning... something.

My parents had violent arguments daily. Mum was absentminded and was always losing things but claimed Dad had stolen it. Dad *was* a kleptomaniac but he had memory problems, so they both believed their own argument. They were ready to fight to the death over a cup or an ornament. You couldn't reason with any of them. You just couldn't argue with Dad. His arguments would be so bizarre and peculiar, you couldn't say anything because you didn't know what the fuck he was on about. He had a favourite saying – apart from calling us fucking cunts, that is. Anything that meant diverging from sitting stock still, not saying a word or being emotionless, our father would say, "Do you think you're a hero?" What the fuck was he talking about? One hot day Sammy took his shirt off. My Dad flew into a rage. "Why have you taken off your shirt? Do you think you're a hero?" Another time Kenny wanted to go to the afternoon football club. Same thing: "Why would you want to do that? Do you think you're a hero? Do you think you're Kenny Dalgleish?" I remember some years later, when I said I wanted to go to University, Dad responded, "Why do you want to go to University? Do you think you're a hero? Or some kind of professor? I know, you think you're Albert Hawkings. You like speaking like a robot, do you?"

What the fuck could I say to that?

I don't think I've ever had an intelligent conversation with my father. My old man's idea of a conversation is he talking, and you listening. He would ring somebody up, talk for half an hour without them getting a word in edgeways. If they replied with a sentence of more than 3 words, he'd say to them, "God, you don't half go on and on."

When Dad was sober, he could be incredibly sweet. He'd make samosas for us to eat. But he made about 30 and would get upset and insecure if you didn't eat them all. He imposed his will on everything, even the food we ate. If I left something on the cooker for a little while, he would add curry powder to it. He'd add it to everything and anything. We told him we didn't like it. He'd counter, "I know fucking best! You're not White, you know!"

It got seriously out of hand. Fucking curry-flavoured angel delight, man.

But it was true – our thinking and character was anglicised. But what do you expect? He didn't bother to teach us our Indian heritage. All we learned was our TV heritage. Dad only taught us to hate. "Why can't you speak any Indian languages? You're not White, y'know." "You didn't teach us, that's why!" I'd usually snap. Actually, that's not completely true. We can swear in Urdu. Those words were easy to learn. Dad said them to us a lot. Sometimes we wanted to say to Dad, "You're not White, y'know!" when he said things like, "Look at these fucking pakis. They should send them back to their own countries. Making things worse for us British." Our Indian father was chocolate-coloured. My Mum pointed this out to him. We kids said under our breaths, "Mum, shut up, please, shut up."

And so they would argue, "You're not White!"

"Yes, I am." Dad would scream.

"You're not English."

"Fucking bitch. You always contradict me!" Slap! Punch! Kick! Kids crying...

For the most part, Dad was a couch potato, but occasionally he'd have a money-making scheme that'd energise him for a week or two. One of Dad's ideas was to sell the flat without telling the council. After watching Antiques Roadshow, he decided to make his fortune by discovering an antique bought dirt-cheap that would sell for thousands. Dad and I went to an auction house in Croydon for a viewing; he had his eyes on an old table. Before the actual auction he had a few drinks. Even though I tried to warn him, he stuck his hand up for things we had no use for, and his reaction to being outbid was to growl, "Fucking cunt!" At the end of the auction, amongst many other things, we left with a lawnmower. As we lived in a flat, it was very useful!

I was learning... something.

Dad decided to make his musical comeback. He contacted the local council who were going to host a Mela, a kind of Asian festival with music and food. He talked about playing to 1000s of people, and he roped Kenny and me as tambourine players. We were too scared to say no. So off we went to Streatham Common to wow people with our dodgy percussion section. As it turned out, people were more interested in modern Indian music so there was only one man and his dog in the audience when we played. I saw that this hurt my father deeply. "They've got no taste!" he bemoaned afterwards. I tried to console him, but he told me to leave him the fuck alone. Dad must have rejected a million instances of genuine love for any kind of fame or attention, which ironically he thought would bring him love.

I spent a lot of my time staring out the living room window. The good things were the colour of the skies, sun and clouds during different parts of the day. I watched a 1001 pass by in my misanthropy; they caused me pain just by walking by. The window overlooked a busy road, the A23, and it had its fair share of accidents. Some of them gave me an adrenaline rush. I was so bored out of my mind and full of hate that I would look forward to the next one. Thankfully, though, most were not fatal; some even managed to get up and walk away from their accident. It didn't take me long to understand my adrenaline rush was very short-lived and those that died stayed dead.

*   *   *   *

As my 16th birthday approached I began looking for a job so I could leave home and start a new life. But who wants to employ a psychotic that left school at 14? In the local paper I came across an ad placed by an organisation called CSV asking for volunteers. In exchange for working away from home as a carer of some sort, you were given bed, board and a little pocket money. This was the perfect solution in my eyes. I applied and was interviewed. They offered me a placement in Manchester, helping a man with cerebral palsy be more independent. I accepted without hesitation.

I was stupid enough to believe that my father would be proud of me for doing this. His response? "I'll kill your mother if you go." A CSV co-ordinator phoned to talk about my placement. Dad picked up the phone; I wasn't in. He asked who it was, and she told him. He decided to tell her all about me, his beloved daughter. He told her I was crazy, violent, a thief, and other nice things. My sister, who overheard the conversation, passed on this information to me. The diminutive confidence I had managed to build up to engage in my new endeavour drained from me like piss from an incontinent. I cried from shame. The next time I spoke to the co-ordinator she told me she didn't take too seriously what my father said because he sounded drunk. I was somewhat relieved but the optimism and excitement was gone. As the day approached for me to leave, the tension in the house was unbearable. Walking down the hallway the same time as my father, he grabbed my hair and slammed my head against the wall. "If you leave, you can never come back. You will never see your family again." Mum wasn't happy about my placement either. "Please don't go, Dolly. Please don't leave me." My younger siblings tugged at me and said the same thing, "Please don't leave us."

The day finally came. I had packed my bags the night before but even then I knew I wouldn't be going. I was too scared to get out of bed. Scared of my father, scared of leaving my family and never seeing them again, scared of starting a new life. I always carried that scared feeling around with me, but that day it was ten times worse. What a horrible feeling to be scared your whole life. I cried for days afterward. Dad had that smirk on his face every time I looked at him, and that made me positively hysterical. That's it, I thought, I'm going to die in this place, either by my father killing me outright or in a thousand and one instalments.

After calming down, I hunted for a job a little closer to home. I didn't need a chaperone when I went out any more. It wasn't that my Dad trusted me. It was just obvious Mum no longer had any free time to go out with me, and my Dad was too lazy to do it himself. I registered with an employment agency in Croydon. They found me a job in a cheese factory in Wimbledon. My first day on the job I wiped the moisture off packaged cheese and then slapped on a sticker. The work was mind numbingly boring and badly paid. I thought if this is what I have to do until I'm 60, I'm fucking committing suicide when I get home. But I didn't kill myself when I got home; I was too tired. I switched on the TV instead.

What I saw in the factory put me off cheese for years. What power or weapons does a minimum wage slave have? Just their bodily fluids. One guy told me he poured his come into a vat. I saw another girl spit on some Brie before wrapping it. I did this job for about 4 weeks before packing it in. I was fed up of smelling like cheese every time I left work.

I quickly found another job as a cashier in Safeways. I hated that fucking job too, being told when I could piss, when I could leave, when I could eat, and being forced to smile while I was being overworked and underpaid. Every cashier the world over knows the bane of carrier bags the customer has to pay for. There would be a least one person every hour that had a hysterical fit about having to pay for bags. Some of them hate pure hate in their eyes. I feared for my life several times. When you tried explaining to them you were just the lowly cashier and didn't make the decisions, they would get even more abusive or pout and refuse to pay for their shopping. It didn't escape my attention that invariably these people didn't mind paying lots of money to kill themselves with drinks, cigarettes and fatty foods. Sometimes I snapped back, "Why don't you officially complain to the people who actually make the decisions?" "I will!" they'd retort. But you knew they never would. While all this was happening, I learned something about humanity. What exactly, I'm not completely sure. But I decided to leave them the fuck alone, something I was unable to do if I was working. I had an argument with a customer. I can't even remember what it was about any more. What I do remember was the customer pointing his finger at me and saying, "I'll have your job!"

"You're fucking welcome to it." When it was my lunch break, I left the store and never returned.

I thought I'd give the 9-5 one more try and found another cashiering job, this time a bit closer to home. I was 2 months into the job when I became ill again. This time my thyroid gland was haemorrhaging. My doctor told me to have a few weeks rest. As it turned out I rested more or less for about a decade after that. I began signing on and enrolled at Lambeth College to do my GCSEs. Because I had kind tutors who didn't treat me like a child, I loved studying there. I met my first two boyfriends there, but in both cases the relationship didn't go far because I was petrified of the idea of them finding out what my father was like. This set the pattern for further relationships. None of them went beyond a certain point. They were all very physical but whenever it got emotional commitment I broke it off. Obviously I had problems with emotional intimacy because of the abuse I grew up with. I'm only questioning and tackling it now in my 30s.

Anyway, one of them phoned me at home (we were still the telephone directory then) and my Dad answered the phone. He thought it was his parental duty to eff and blind at the poor guy and threaten to kill him. Oh shit, I thought, please let him stay on the phone forever so he won't come after me. Dad slammed the phone down and glared at me with spittle coming out the sides of his mouth. "Who is this guy? Are you fucking whoring, just like your mother? I can't believe it, my daughter is a prostitute!" I tried denying knowledge of the guy who just phoned. It was no good. I was beaten by his walking stick – which was less a mobility aid and more of a street weapon – and locked in my room. It was back to peeing in jars again. Unable to leave by the door, there was only one other way to escape the room and the situation – and that was by window. It didn't matter to me if we were on the 3rd floor. Actually, that was a plus. I sat on the outside sill. Should I jump? Or should I get high on life? I chose to endure more humiliations of my beautiful life.

There were two reasons for this. One, we gained two more dogs after Bobby. We didn't have to buy dogs number two and three. A neighbour had locked a dog in their balcony for a few days, letting it bark for hours on end. My Dad and Sheila went downstairs to ask why the dog was locked out. The neighbour said somebody had given her the dog but she didn't really want it. My Dad said he would take her, and they brought her up. She was a small brown mongrel dog who looked a bit like a fox; her name was Sheba. She was underweight and dirty too. Bobby went to sniff her but she snapped at him. She was extremely timid and defensive, hiding under furniture and only coming out to eat. When I took her for walks she would dash under a parked car if somebody walked by us. It was obvious somebody had beaten her into this submissive state. She was like that for almost a year, but with love and patience she slowly came out of her shell and her true nature began to show, that of a crazy little motherfucker. She liked picking fights with the toughest dogs on the street, dogs that were three times the size of her. She loved life; she loved chasing flies around the house. She would enter a room full of people to fart and then leave. When the 'ping' of the microwave timer rang, she ran straight into the kitchen and insisted she be fed. She loved her food. She had 2 sets of puppies, which we sold. It tore me up not knowing to what kind of homes we were selling the puppies to. My Dad just didn't think about things like that. He just liked to think how great he was whilst the world he made screamed and cried around him. We kept one of Sheba's pups and named her Ginger for obvious reasons. She was even crazier than her Mum. When she was no more than 5 inches high, she dragged a bunch of bananas from the kitchen to the living room to snack upon. I loved our dogs so much that I couldn't really entertain suicide even if I was seriously depressed. The second reason was that I discovered James Dean. I watched 'Rebel Without A Cause' and it just blew me away. I knew keenly what Jim Stark was going through because of the rejection of his peers. I cried when his character made a joke in the observatory and nobody laughed. But he was the hero of the film, he made being the rebel, the loner cool. And of course he was a very horny motherfucker. He became some one to emulate. He gave me something to do day in and day out as I acted out his scenes and tried to generally be like him. My walls were covered with his posters. I came to believe that I could talk to him for real, and we had some amazing conversations about art and life. It was obvious that I was able to talk to the dead; the living were making no sense... This lasted for a good few years. I read up all about him. When I read he died at 24 I was both saddened and jealous. He lived fast and died young. He had no time for the 9-5, which I admired. I was beginning to see the 9-5 as a shit and spoon race. People were taking part in a stupid race attempting to balance the shit of work, mortgages, bills and consumerism on a spoon, thinking 'I mustn't drop this. I have to win this race, I have to get ahead.' They were proud to be winners in a shit and spoon race. I wanted nothing of it.

Unfortunately I had to deal with social security and job centre clerks. They lost me forever when they didn't even bother to ask me what kind of job interested me. I was the shit on their shoe and they let me know it. Do they have to pass a sarcasm aptitude test before they are offered the job? But I heard worst shit from my father so I was able to take the belittling and cruel interviews every six months from them.

This was the pattern until I was about 21, alternating between depressions and psychosis, daytime TV and violent arguments. This was best typified by our doorbell that we owned during this time: it was a musical kind that played annoying songs. Dad didn't bother to replace the battery until it was well and truly dead. So every time the button was pressed, a very discordant 'There's No Place Like Home' whined and slurred its song. I had grown out of my James Dean obsession and was basically looking for a new hobby. I was still somewhat depressed but it wasn't so bad: I was only thinking of suicide 10 times a day rather than the usual 1000 times. My Dad was still as fucked up as ever, and this time he had a new obsession: hoarding. Actually, come to think of it, most of our furniture came from skips and rubbish tips. It wasn't frugality but a compulsion. The hoarding situation got so bad, you could get lost in a room. We were forced to use fewer bedrooms so they'd be more room to accommodate junk, forced to share beds with each other and we weren't kids any more. After an argument with Sheila, he threw away her bed and filled her room with rubbish. She was forced to sleep on the sofa. He'd bring home chairs with 3 legs. You just couldn't reason with him. "It's an antique, I'll fix it." He'd argue. He insisted on keeping a crappy hi-fi system that broke in the early 80s well into the 21st century. "I'll fix it," Attempting to raise the point that the company no longer existed nor did the parts to fix it triggered a strange violence. "Don't fucking contradict me!"

There was a magazine I was reading at the time called SKY. They had a pen pal section in the back pages and I put an ad in it; I received over 200 replies. It took me all day to go properly through them and choose whom I was going to reply to; it felt great. About 30 or so letters came from perverts and psychos. I remember one guy telling me to send him a photo of me sitting on a swing in a see-through blouse! In the end, I replied to about 12 letters from those who intrigued me the most. Over the years I slowly lost touch with most of them but there was one person who inspired me to take a new direction in life, a guy called Adrian Gill. He talked about the novel he was writing and I thought that was pretty cool. I liked writing stories and poems but most ended up in the bin because I didn't take it seriously. I never considered writing a novel but Adrian planted the idea in my head. It was around about this time I discovered the Beat Writers, such as William Burroughs, Allen Ginsberg and Jack Kerouac, quite accidentally. There was a book in the library that kept catching my eye and wouldn't refuse to let go until I picked up the book and took it out; it was Allen Ginsberg's biography. This introduction to the Beats changed my life. These were people who wrote the way they lived, and lived the way they wrote. They wrote from the soul and not the intellect. I wanted to be like them. They could care less about craft and form and all the other things that send me to sleep. I started reading all their books, and they all had an intoxicating effect on my soul. My depression lifted. Especially after reading On The Road by Jack Kerouac. Now I wanted to be a free spirit too, like a bird. But someone was taking pot shots at me.

One of my Dad's agents, Mrs Warren, sent me to a couple of auditions, and I got offered a small TV part both times. And both times, my father phoned the agent and said he didn't want me doing them and pulled me out of the projects by telling the casting people I had to look after a sick grandfather. I was enraged, anger lifted me a good few inches off the ground, but at the same time I didn't know how to stand up to my father. Every day I found I could hate my father a little bit more. Here was another example of him being jealous of his own children. Anything I wanted to do, he hijacked and sabotaged "because," he said, "I know what's best for you." Another example of this happened not too long after.

One of my Mum's favourite programs was Strike It Lucky, the game show hosted by Michael Barrymore, and she wanted to go on it. She wanted to press the button to reveal the prizes on the TV screen, and me to answer the questions. I sent off the application and went to the audition, not expecting us to be picked. But they wanted more disabled people on the show, so they *did* pick us. We didn't tell my Dad at first, but somehow he got wind of it, and unknown to us wrote to Michael Barrymore, begging him for a chance to showcase his comedy on Strike It Lucky.

One the day they were shooting the show, a car picked us up to take us to the studio. We had a rehearsal in the morning and then we were ushered into a room for lunch. They laid out a nice spread, but my Mum and me were too nervous to eat.

Before the actual shooting, we had to have our makeup done. The lady who did me had been drinking on the job and painted my face a fluorescent shade of orange. Finally it was time to shoot the actual show.

Michael Barrymore did his rounds of contestant introductions; my Mum and I were the last ones to be introduced. Michael asked my Mum how to sign 'I love you', and she showed him. Then all of a sudden my Dad called out from the audience. Michael asked my father to come down, and my Dad muscled in front of the camera.

He introduced himself as Chicko Patel, and then told a few jokes, one of them being that his favourite food was curry and chips, and then he left to rejoin my sisters in the audience.

I had been pretty calm when they started filming, however my Dad's intrusion had utterly thrown me. I got easy answers wrong and totally forgot the aim of the game was to bank prizes. We didn't win, but made some good money out of it, and we were able to pay off a few debts. After the filming, drinks were made available. My father drank so much he could barely stand. A studio car took us home.

Again I was enraged with my father. He would even pull the light away from us or publicly insult us just to have his five minutes of fame. It reminded me of the times he took our sports trophies and taped his name over ours, and then showed them off.

When the show was televised a few months later, I prayed that there was something better on the other side and only a handful of people would watch the game show. I cringed as I watched it my Dad act the fool and me be a child of a fool. I didn't want to go out unless I had a paper bag over my head. "We don't have any paper bags, just plastic ones." The local shopkeeper said. Ah man, a plastic bag was even better. But in the end I did go out, and in the end people did point and laugh at me. Life was just full of joy, and the world full of laughter.

Like a small sponge in a million gallons of watery shit, I just soaked all this up. I began dreaming about killing my father, but I knew I wouldn't have the guts to do it. So I turned the hate inward, and my body reacted and psychosomatic symptoms showed themselves. From head to foot, something was affected, generally weakness down my left side, pins and needles, and loss of balance and hearing. I was sent to St Thomas Hospital for tests. I was convinced I had MS was going to die. I wanted to die. In the end, they found out the pins and needles were caused by me taking too much of my thyroxine medication, and so that was easily eradicated, but no cause could be found for the other symptoms. When the depression was finally tackled, the weakness went too. But I still have problems with balance and hearing. On my last visit to the neurology dept in the early 90s I saw a new doctor. He took one look at me and prescribed me anti-depressants. I also left with the diagnosis of being 'clinically depressed'.

My siblings were suffering in their own way too. I guess Paula had enough of it, and ran away from home when she was 17. Mum went hysterical and needed to be calmed down. Can you believe it, Dad was actually puzzled as to why she ran away. "There's no problems in the family." He told a police officer who came to the flat to interview us about Paula's disappearance. I think this cop could spot a bullshitter a mile off because it was obvious he didn't believe my Dad. The house was full of junk and dog shit. Dad couldn't be bothered most days to take the dogs out and banned us from taking them out too. The policeman saw this. He asked my Dad were Paula slept. Dad showed him the ratty mattress on the floor as if it were absolutely normal place to sleep. The copper reported my father to social services. DSS clerks may have to take sarcasm aptitude tests to get their jobs but too many social workers learn to be apathetic and redundant. They came to the flat for God knows what reason, because they didn't ask to see Paula, who came back home a few weeks after she ran off, to ask what she thought or why she ran away. They didn't ask to see any of us separate from our father; they asked me about Dad's violence with him in the same room. In fact, Dad had coached me what to say, and I said it, because if I had told the truth, would social services have saved the day? Now that *is* fucking funny.

I took refuge in writing. I poured my soul into poetry. Looking back now, I can't tell any more whether it is poetry or psychosis. You decide...

A heart inside a sun inside an empty universe... empty chairs capture the essence of the soul... I want to feel something – self-service ECT – on the other hand – a razor will also get blood out of the stone – until my cup overflows – hell for leather; I have torn up suicide notes for skin – see this straitjacket, well used, abused, almost torn at the seams... 3 a.m. is silence's dirty caller – leaving obscene messages on the answering machine of my mind – salvation in impotence... Why is the world full of purple Santa Clauses playing syphilitic pinball – the walls are turning into clouds – and the window has become a sun – the brain is a strange instrument; it receives endless messages of pain, but the horrible thing about it is that it's sometimes the sender too – not unlike making dirty and threatening phone calls to yourself – and this poem is one of them... I woke up before the sun rose – thoughts of suicide were my alarm clock in those early hours – suicide was a comfortable bed – a sleep that actually slept – a sun that didn't burn you as it offered your lonely world light – well, that morning, I wanted death more than daytime TV. But my gun was in another room, far away, and as I am a lazy person, and as my cowardice has a beautiful star, I waited for the sun to rise instead... I am God inside the body of a nobody – but then again, aren't we all? These voices get my undivided attention. They dictate my suicide note to me on the most beautiful of days – poetic justice – they tear my mind apart; they rent out my mind to dead souls, dead souls that were happy to be dead... I feel mutilated by life, violated by living – the only high I want to be is six feet deep... To be tortured and tortured and tortured and not allowed to die – that's life for you, and it feels absolutely beautiful...

Sometimes I didn't even name the poems; I just called them suicide note number 1, 2, 3, etc. For example, this poem is called suicide note no.1: People say life is too short – I say the nights are too long – I can't and don't sleep any more – Yeah, right, you sneer, you have to sleep, otherwise your body and mind wouldn't be able to cope – You're right; I concur wholeheartedly – the body and mind *can't* cope. But I am still alive, still breathing.

Insomnia is not a life-threatening condition unfortunately. It merely drives you insane – with the help of 101 other things, of course – Insomnia has a certain art to it, though – there's a certain amount of grace in lasting the dawn without killing yourself or someone else. It may be a futile, superfluous, banal grace, but it's grace nonetheless – sunrise slithers like a snake and eats you whole – suicide notes are easy to write...

...but consoling letters a little harder. The family received a letter from our Grandpa from Scotland. Our Nan, our Mum's stepmother, had yet another stroke; this one leaving her totally immobilised. Granddad just couldn't give her the specialised care she needed, so she was cared for by the local hospital. You could tell this broke his heart. He visited her almost every day. My Mum wanted to go to Scotland to visit them both. Although I wasn't emotionally up for it, I went too. I wrote Grandpa a letter saying we'd visit him to help him out.

Grandpa welcomed us with a stressed smile. I was hypersensitive to his pain, so much so I wanted to chicken out of visiting my Nan. When I suggested to Grandpa we visit Glasgow as a day out before visiting Nan, he understandably blew his top. "You said you wanted to help, but this is no helping me at all!" I backed down and went to see our Nan. Nana Adelaide was the embodiment of a kindly grandmother, sweet natured, spoiling us kids rotten. I never heard her utter a word in anger. She and Grandpa had taken a couple of holidays to Blackpool with us and we had great times. She kept buying us things when Grandpa wasn't looking. We went to the part of the hospital where the long-term residents stayed. When I saw Nana I was so shocked I almost burst into tears; I had to swallow a few times to regain composure. She looked ten years older. Her facial expressions of happiness, kindness and laughter we stolen from her by the stroke - her face was an immobile mask. She wanted to speak to us but was only able to moan and slur. The face was incapable of expressing an emotion but you could tell by her eyes she was upset at not being able to speak. Tears kept welling in her eyes, drowning me. Grandpa went to hug her and it caused her psychical pain. That ripped my heart into blood-soaked confetti. I'm sure she felt like an exhibit that was unable to tell people to piss off and leave her alone. I visited her about 3 times, learning more and more about pain. It is a teacher that edifies the facts of life in a foreign language - or it is one boring word repeated a million times – the mantra of the razor blade. Pain. Pain. Pain. Pain. Pain. Pain. Sick of it yet?

Pain doesn't care if you're sick of it. It just keeps on coming. This time an uncle ended up in hospital, a psychiatric ward, in fact. He thought my father was evil, a demon, so he was diagnosed schizophrenic. "He's fucking crazy," Dad said. But I didn't think so. There was a lot of sense to what my uncle said...

Pain, pain, pain, pain...

Life. Life. Life. Life. Life. Life. Life. Life. Sick of it yet?

Yes, I was sick of it. I was in my own toxic little bubble, unable to reach out to anyone, and no one able to reach out to me. Suffocating slowly, slowly suffocating, while the TV was on. I had my father's slurred insults and the demonic auditory hallucination competing for my thinking space, fuck that, competing for my soul, so I went into my bedroom with a razor blade like it was a cup of tea. Once under the covers, I slit my wrists, and let the warm blood become a blanket to a perpetual slumber. I didn't expect to wake up. I didn't want to wake up. Of course I did wake up, otherwise a ghost is writing this. Shit, there's a lot of sense to that…

I woke up my T-shirt and sheets stained with blood, but I was alive. I looked at the gaping wounds on my wrists. Obviously I hadn't cut deep enough, and I had cut horizontally when I should have made a vertical incision. At least I got a good night's sleep. Intermittently after that I self-mutilated to relieve stress. For what was my soul but a skin shed by a tortured, lost animal? My self-mutilation phase only lasted about a month though. Self-mutilation just doesn't go deep enough, I found. I may have got bored with it, but my scars don't seem to have got bored off me yet. Sometimes when people shake my hand, they see the heart on the sleeve and the scars on my wrist, and their demeanour changes instantly: they shrink away from me. You smile, but they will never look you in the eye again.

The DSS sent me to an organisation in the London Bridge area, which specialised in getting disabled people back into work. The co-ordinator listened to everybody's hopes, dreams and ambitions and then, with a laugh, dismissed them. "You as disabled people," she said, "cannot afford to aim high. I'm sorry but that's the way of the world." When I told her I wanted to be a writer, she smirked. "I'm sorry, but you're being a little bit ridiculous there, aren't you?" She lost me at that moment. "Society cannot accommodate you as a writer." She said. Since when has using your intelligence and creativity been an act of wilful disobedience towards society? I think it was a ten-week course, but I left it after a week. I knew the DSS were probably going to stop my benefits, so I planned my suicide by jumping out of the window. As before, my dogs sensed something was wrong and began howling and whining. There were five dogs in the flat now. When they humped each other, Dad said, "Leave them, it's only nature." It was also natural for 8 puppies to be the end product. We sold six and kept two because we had no more buyers, giving us a total of five. I had taken over the looking after of the dogs by this time. They were my babies, and I couldn't leave them behind in a world that had my Dad in it. So once again, I chose life with a wry smile.

I went to the local library to read up on benefits, and took a chance by claiming disability benefits. My application was successful, so it meant no more going to the local dole office to observe humanity being beautiful, or having to read the ridiculous script society concocted about wanting to work and taking orders from other people. I always leave dole or job interviews wanting to kill myself or piss myself with laughter. Not that I was lazy, or am lazy. I currently (2002) work about 70-80 hours a week at my various projects and love it. But if somebody offered me a minimum wage job working under some arsehole, watch my face change colour and my hand turn into a one-fingered gesture. Why do I feel so strongly about this? I could come up with moral, political or philosophical arguments about this, but I just believed I was too good for it. It was beneath my station. That and being as hypersensitive as a hiccupping haemophiliac shaving himself. I'm more like my father than I'd like to admit. I swung from feelings of superiority to inadequacy on a daily basis, like a smiling dead clown on a swinging noose.

I kept my contact with humans to a minimum, and with good reason to sometimes. Discrimination because of my mental illness was rife. The worst incident I can remember happened at my local post office. There was a post office clerk there that was a bit of a bastard to everyone. Giving people their benefits caused him great pain. One time he asked me why I was on benefits. I told him it was because of mental illness. "What a waste of money," he said, "Hitler had the right idea about you people." That upset so much I cried for days.

Discrimination doesn't only come from strangers. There were certain people in the Asian community who told me to keep quiet about my mental health problems. I knew this was because the community

103

already felt marginalized and demonised. By being mentally ill and part of the Asian community was seen as more than an embarrassment. One statistic racists like to throw at people is that ethnic minorities are more likely to have long-term mental health problems, as if it were some intrinsic genetic abnormality. Yes, ethnic minorities are more likely to be ill – in the UK, that is. In their own country they are *less* likely to have long mental problems than their Anglo-Saxon counterparts. It is the prejudice, isolation, bad housing and unemployment ethnic minorities are more likely to experience that triggers and exacerbates mental distress. So I understand why certain non-whites don't want anything to bring negative attention to the community. But this puts the mentally ill non-white in a world of pain, a world where they are the only inhabitant. I think paranoia is justified for some non-whites, who get verbal abuse and shit put through their letterbox because of their colour. I know of one person who was driven to suicide because of this.

Fuck everyone, I thought to myself, I am going to be the greatest writer alive, and set about writing my first novel. Heavily influenced by Jack Kerouac's 'On The Road' and fuelled by mania, I wrote day and night. I wanted the book to be an autobiographical travelogue but I didn't have enough travel experience for that, well, not on this planet, anyway, so I padded it with wishes and fiction. It took me about 6 weeks to complete it, because I had to start again several times. The book was called 'DEVIATIONS' and the first page had the definition of the word: wanderings; divergences from a set course; departure; digressions. I wrote about how I wanted to live, with as little contact with bureaucracy and the rat race as possible, forever on the road because no place was good enough to stop for. When I finished the book, my mania went even higher. Days lasted for centuries; I had gone to the sun and back. I had changed world history, shuffling figures around like a chess game. I was utterly convinced the book was one of the greatest ever written and that it could save the world and de-program minds. I went on a spending spree because I was certain the book would make me a millionaire overnight. So I was puzzled as to why I was getting rejection slips from publishers. I thought they were too brainwashed to see the book's greatness. I asked a couple of people whose opinion I respected what they thought of it. They thought it was good but needed a lot of working on. They both said the dialogue was not naturalistic enough and some of the language was too Americanised. What the hell was dialogue? I didn't have much personal experience of it, not unless you include my conversations with gods and demons. It was constructive criticism from them but I fell into a deep depression because of it nonetheless. I didn't go back to the novel until 2001, when it went through a rewrite and became more true to life; the dialogues were modelled on real people this time. The depression following the writing of the book the first time round lasted about a year. If I can't write, I might as well be dead, I told myself. I didn't need to pray at night as I was able to hear the prayers of the dead to God, some of them screaming at him for the pain to stop. Even listening to their lamentations were preferable to listening to the thoughts in my own head: '*I can't do anything right. What right did I think I had to be a writer? Everybody must be laughing at the way I wrote the book, just like they laugh when they hear me speak. I'm just a thing to laugh at - that is my role in this world. Why do people move away from me on the bus? I must smell or be so horrifically ugly people can't take being on the same planet as me. Stop laughing at me, Satan! Stop laughing at me, God! It says a lot about life that the Devil and God laugh at the same thing. Nobody loves me, not even my family. They wish I were dead and out of their lives. I am evil and contaminate anything that looks at me. I can't do anything right. Why am I letting myself live? The pain in my body is too big for my skin, maybe I should cut it open and let it all seep out. I want to cut the eyes out of my head so the world won't hurt as much. Nobody loves me. Would death even want me or would it spit me out like a bad seed? I should kill myself, what's the point in living like this? I want to die but I'm too scared to. See, I can't do anything right. I am evil, evil, evil, evil, evil, evil. Please, God, Don't let me wake up to another fucking day. I can't do anything right. Every second of my life I regret. The future will only promise more regrets and more instances to exercise cowardice. Mum should have had an abortion...*' This caustic commentary I listened to every night for hours on end until I was exhausted enough to sleep. They were there when I woke up, paralysing me so much I was incapable of lifting my head off the pillow. My second novel 'The New Day' was more or less a transcript of these thoughts.

A year after I wrote 'Deviations' I began my second book. Mania had given my first book the necessary fuel for it to stay on the road. An energised depression kept my second book going. This book, called 'The New Day' wasn't going to have a happy ending. In fact, there wasn't going to be any happiness anywhere in the fucking thing. The story centred on a woman called Donna, who books into a seedy hotel 'The New Day'. Finding each and every new day a painful and sordid place to be, Donna decides to check out permanently in the form of suicide. The conflict arises when her estranged husband arrives on the scene to frustrate her heinous quest. Although she has more than enough reasons to commit suicide, it is the thing that's supposed to save her which finally gives her the impetus to commit suicide – love. It was a speculative, philosophical book, the prose inspired by my dark thoughts and nocturnal depressive rambling. Because of my depression, this book took longer to write, about 6 months. I didn't even bother submitting this book to publishers. Then in a month-long period of mania I wrote a novella about a female serial killer. I have noticed that all my books are about outsiders trying to take control of their lives, to regain what they perceive to be taken away from them, even if it was sometimes negative control.

By this time I was fed up of writing. My psychiatric social worker suggested I join a work project for people with mental health difficulties and learning disabilities called Feathers (now First Step Trust). He gave me the hard sell about it being a supportive environment where there was a variety of interesting work to do. I didn't know anyone else who was mentally ill and was feeling lonely, so I said yes.

I went to their place in Kennington and was interviewed and showed around. They had various work projects going – a painting and decorating team, a gardening team, a cleaning section, a print room, and a craft section. The print room and art section looked interesting to me so I choose to a voluntary worker there. It was approaching Christmas, so I helped make seasonal decorations, like small Christmas trees. I enjoyed myself there and learned a lot of new skills such as how to use a computer, but I was still incredibly shy and only talked to a few people there. We were only paid a couple of quid a week but I liked that. I felt that if people gave me lots of money, it was like they owned me. I stayed there for a couple of months before leaving because things were deteriorating at home and Mum wanted me with her to protect her from Dad's violence. I was angry with both of them for sabotaging any attempt of mine to live my own life. My mind had its own insidious mantra to keep my black heart satisfied: 'He has to die. He has to die.'

Sammy worked as a model for a schoolbook. When the money came through to his agent, Dad told her to make out the cheque to him. Sammy earned about £2000 for that and didn't see a penny of it. Dad spent it all. Sammy was enraged; he had made plans with that money, and had a big argument with Dad. "You're a bastard," Sammy said. "How dare you speak to your father like that! You're still a child, it's up to me what I do with that money! I have to pay the fucking bills, you know." We all had our breaking points with Dad and that was Sammy's. Sam knew the money went on drink, because we were still getting the final demands of bills that hadn't been paid for months, and in some cases years even.

Things just seemed to get worse and worse. Everybody in the family was angry or depressed. I couldn't see any happy endings or ways out. Death or daytime TV was my choice every time I woke. I had no motivation to get up and commit suicide. With living you just needed to sit there.

Dad verbally abused his agent for not giving him work. But it was to be expected; his behaviour on set was getting from bad to worse. One of the last jobs the agent gave us was on a Spanish production. Sheila, Paula, Dad and I went. There was a makeup worker there whose gender wasn't easily recognisable and she received quizzical glances from those who passed her. My Dad weaved drunkenly towards her and said, "Are you a man or a woman?" "I'm a pre-op male to female transsexual." With a piece of pork chop in his moustache, Dad said to her, "You people disgust

109

me." Called to the set, we were shoppers in a real supermarket. After a few takes they got fed up of my father. "Take 1. Action!" Pssst. My father opened a can of lager. "CUT!" "Take 2." "You fucking cunt!" Dad said to his unruly shopping trolley. "CUT!" "Take 3!" CRASH! Dad mowed down a shopping display. My father was told he was no longer needed. Again, we got those looks of pity or disgust for having him as a father we were so used to. Sheila and I went back to work; we had to browse the grocery part of the shop. In the middle of shooting I heard my Dad call, "Oi, Dolly. Quickly put these oranges in your bag!" He stumbled into the shot with an armful of stolen oranges. I think that day I understood my father was in his own unreachable little world. We could do fuck all to draw him out. Not that I wanted to any more. I was getting lost in my own world of increasing depression, despair and laughing demons. I would sit in a chair all day, waiting hopelessly for my hopeful death.

I tried claiming for Incapacity Benefit. As I said I wasn't well enough to work, I had to see a DSS doctor. The whole procedure was horrible, the outcome decided before I even stepped foot into his office. I had nobody to help me: Dad was in his own little world, Mum deaf, social services saying they couldn't help. I was told later I should have brought along a lawyer or qualified welfare worker to put forward my case. But how the hell was I supposed to do that when I was barely able to hold a conversation or write a letter. I had tried phoning a help line, but I would invariably stand there with the receiver in my hand not knowing what to do next.

So I was only able to give monosyllabic answers to the doctor's complicated and longwinded questions. One question I remember: What does your depression stop you from doing? I can see now it stopped me from being able to understand the question or to answer it coherently. My actual answer: 'I dunno.'

He had a form in front of him and in the box for that question, he put N/A.

The doctor was no fool. He knew exactly how my depression was affecting me just by looking at me. But he didn't care about that. The DSS were squeezing his balls to do their bidding, to save them money, in effect to abandon this being in need. Is it any wonder I – and most other severe depressives - felt like the whole world doesn't care?

He was just like his pen pushing counterparts in the dole office. There were a few decent dole office clerks, but most looked down their noses at you. It wasn't until I got out of the depression that I saw these people for what they were – spiritless, unimaginative, petty little bureaucrats. I dread to think what the world would be like if they made up all the rules. Fuck, they *do* make up all the rules!

Out of the blue, Dad got a phone call from Barrymore's producer, inviting him to do a 5-minute comedy spot on the show Barrymore. Dad was elated. "This is it," he punched the air. "This is the big time. I'll probably get offered my own show! I'm gonna be rich!" We tried telling him not to get too carried away, but he'd reply, "You're always putting me down. You don't want me to succeed." We wanted to be happy for him but we knew it would all end in tears – ours and his.

I was in the audience with my Mum and sisters, not really wanting to be there. Comedy is the fool's gold and we knew Dad would make a fool of himself, which meant more people would point and laugh at us when we walked down the street in our hometown. Soon it was time for Dad to come on: he walked down the stairs looking like a bemused holidaymaker. "Is this TWA?" he asked. I laughed; maybe it'll be okay, I told myself. Dad's eyes were glazed over; he was obviously drunk. I should have expected it. When I had gone with my father to showbiz functions, it was always the comedians that drank the hardest and snorted the most coke. Laughter is a strange language. Being funny and being happy isn't the same thing. And I think some comedians get confused by that. Dad played up the Asian stereotype, wobbling his head and laying on a thick accent. "My name is Chicko Patel." He took his socks and shoes off and began cutting his toenails. I cringed with shame. I hated my body for not being able to disappear. I didn't laugh for a full month after that moment. My Dad was teaching me that laughter was just too fucking painful. After the show, he got even drunker. When he sobered up he expected adulation, all he got were sniggers and complaints from Asian newspapers about his racist rendition of a Patel. I could tell he was crushed by this reaction but he tried to brush it off. "These

Patels have no sense of fucking humour. They should be glad I'm making their name famous." His expectations of more fame and fortune also came to nothing. "People don't have any sense of humour nowadays," he complained. "I'm a great comedian." Later on, he would cry in his room. Only his alcoholism had the biggest smile. I think Woody Allen said, "Tragedy plus time equals comedy." But it works the other way around too: "Comedy plus time equals tragedy…"

I felt like my life had become a tragedy, I thought I was a waste of space better off dead. When I passed laughing people on the street, I was sure it was me that was amusing them with my gauche and inept being. I woke up at noon and went to bed a 6pm, wakefulness was something to get rid off. I was unable to read or write coherently; even watching TV was too taxing. Life-affirming daytime TV just made me homicidal. I sat in an armchair for the whole day, wanting to die but with not enough energy to do anything about it. The only constructive thing I was doing was helping out at the deaf club my Mum went to. There was a social worker there, and I would beg her to help me get a council flat so I could get away from my Dad. She said she couldn't really help me because I wasn't deaf, although she did speak to my GP about my needing counselling and donated a cooker when I did finally get my own flat. But then in my morose state, I said to myself, "Here you go, Dolly, another rejection. You're only born to be rejected by every single human being on the planet."

I had to see my GP every six weeks. Every consultation was the same: "Still feeling depressed?" "Yes," "Still want to die?" "Yes," His usual response: "I'm going to increase/change your antidepressant." He would tell me my life was precious, but then prescribe me the cheapest drug. I loved my irony. They should make it in tablet form. But in some ways it was lucky they were cheap because at my most depressed I couldn't be bothered to take them. Again my parents weren't there to help me out; they just spent their time looking for more ways to hate each other. This went on for about a year, I think. Then the GP surgery had a resident counsellor and I was referred to her.

Her name was Rachel Murray. I really appreciated her warm-heartedness but in the long run counselling did little to assuage my chronic depression. It was less about counselling and more about having somebody that cared about me. Anyway, our session didn't last very long and I was acutely aware of this. I would be just beginning to open up when I was told the session was over. I felt like I was wheeled into surgery and opened up, and then wheeled straight out because of time constraints. I left the counselling sessions with an open gaping psychic wound, and told I would be seen in a fortnight. When I got to know more people who used the psychiatric system, that would be one of the main banes: feeling like you were on a conveyer belt and rushed through appointments. Rachel said to me to use the sessions to clean out the wound that was stopping me have a productive life, and sometimes the sessions did some psychic hoovering. But once I returned home, I found there was a vacuum my father was happy to fill with his psychopathic phlegm.

I had regular arguments with God. I told him off for creating pain and paedophilia, death and my Dad. I said things like: "If you don't kill my Dad, I'll never speak to you again." But my Dad would wake up the next day, and I would speak to God again, if only to complain to him over a celestial customer service desk that was my insomnia. Even though I no longer believed in God, I had to do something. Insomnia was the thing that taught me hell could always get a little bit worse. To endure a day of hell and then not being able to find escape in sleep was like sleeping on a bed of razors, and I woke up absolutely shredded by the experience. One day I recorded onto tape my insomnia: you hear tossing and turning, silent sobs, and ruminations: "The brain is a strange thing; it believes its own lies eventually... When we die, we all go to hell, both the good and the bad... There won't be a speedy Armageddon, an instant Armageddon like instant coffee. It's going to be slow and painful. Maybe I should speed it up along, get the whole fucking thing over with... The pain of the rising sun... I still feel like dying, but my day is being taken over by practicalities, like wiping my arse after I take a shit... I only hear from the world when it needs money off me..." Another night I repeated the words: "I sense the dimming of the light," what must have been 10,000 times until dawn. I would take the occasional real razor to bed as the ultimate sleeping pill. Yet the morning sun would redeem me somewhat. As I've said in one of my poems, 'My cowardice has a beautiful star'. The razor was only slightly harder to swallow than life.

One day a letter came for me. I hated opening letters; they usually told me I owed somebody something. I didn't know my cheap life could be so expensive. It got so bad that it would take me an hour to pluck the courage to open it. When I finally did open it, a smile formed on my face. It was from the local council offering me and Sheila a two bed roomed flat. I had applied with Sheila when I was 16. I wanted to apply for a one bed roomed flat but I was told I would get a flat quicker if applied with someone else. I now know that not to be true. I was almost 26 when that letter came. But it wasn't the new beginning I hoped it would be. It was only a five-minute walk away from my parent's place, and whenever I spent time at my new place, Dad always visited in a drunken state, sometimes abusive, scaring the kids that played outside. It upset me that I couldn't escape my father. He was like a monkey on my back, a fucking fat monkey. Sheila and Paula also lived at the new flat, but because I was tidy and organised and they were not, we argued a lot. In the end, I had to run two households, which stressed me out. Suicide seemed to offer more luxurious accommodation. New neighbours moved into the flat above us in Adare Walk, and they brought with them a karaoke machine. Listening to them sing out of tune

Boyzone songs changed my suicidal impulse into a homicidal one. The neighbours at my Mum's place were no better. Because of my Dad's constant verbal abuse, they complained to the council, who in turn threatened the whole family with eviction. We were being punished for our father's misdemeanours too. This fuelled my paranoia like a Molotov cocktail.

1997 began. I no longer looked to the New Year as new but more of the same old shit. The only times I went out was to take the dogs for a walk, help Mum with the shopping, or see my GP to tell him how beautiful my life was. Sammy recently had bought a new car. While everyone else complimented it, I was wondering how long it would take me to gas myself in it. I told Rachel, my counsellor about this. "How about your dogs, you don't want to leave them behind." She said, knowing I loved my dogs. "Oh, they're coming with me." I told her. She notified my GP about this, and my GP in turn referred me to Crisis Intervention at Lewin Road, Streatham's Community Mental Health Centre. I went there with the GP's letter in my hand, not knowing what to expect. I was a bit worried about being whisked away to a mental hospital and having the key thrown away. But then again I was so apathetic that emotion didn't last longer than a fart.

The mental health centre was on a residential road, and it was a house rather than a purpose built clinic. I met with Chris Hart, who interviewed me. I remember telling him I saw little point in going on. Another day just meant another argument from Dad, and another bill from the rest of the world. I also confided in him that I felt my Mum and Dad looked to me as the parent, that they expected me to clean up the messes they made. My Dad threw tantrums and my Mum was too scared to do anything on her own so was therefore dependant on me. Going to bed at night never brought respite but its own hell. Suicide was another spoilt brat I was the guardian of, which kept tugging at me for the slightest attention. I spent whole nights resisting suicide. I felt I was being driven to kill myself because sometimes I didn't want to die. My black suicidal depression was always waiting in the wings, laughing whenever the skies turned grey.

I told Chris I took two O.D.s in 1995, and one in 1996. Death didn't come for me then, it just made fun of me by stuffing me into a bottle of nauseous pain and painful nausea. I also showed him the scars of slashed wrists, another failure. I was asked what my daily activities consisted of. I told him a bit of housework and a lot of TV. I was a cabbage.

What did I look like to other people: overweight, wearing the same clothes day in, day out, rarely smiling or making eye contact, always looking at the ground, or sitting hunched over. Oh, also a history of self-harm, so don't forget the many happy scars on my arms. Chris was easy to speak to. I was a suicidal parrot, repeating again and again that I wanted to die. He never chided me, but gently steered me towards another subject. We agreed a safety plan, which was that I'd contact him if I had thoughts of self-harming during the day. At night, if I was feeling suicidal, I was to lock the windows (because I liked the idea of stepping out into the world through my parent's 3rd floor window), tell someone how I felt, and if necessary, call an ambulance. I said yes to this but I knew if the suicidal feeling was big enough the paper this was written on was just toilet paper for my shitty life and shitty death.

I saw more of Chris. He asked me to write a diary of my thoughts, hoping to show me how a negative attitude taints thoughts. I wrote a diary every day for a month. Here are some excerpts:

I wake up, feeling dark, dull and desolate. I see the day as waking up to a futile struggle against financial and family problems. The D.S.S have sent me off to a job interview I have absolutely no interest in. I hate when this happens. It makes me feel like I have no control in my life

Went out for a walk through Battersea Park to blow off steam. The sun helped lift my mood and the clouds rolling over the trees calmed me. When the sun shines through the greyness; it infuses me with a life-giving substance. But the depressing train ride home deflates me; I feel people are talking about me behind my back. My life is unexciting and vapid again, like any variance would be outside my emotional and financial means...

Waking up, the day ahead seems pointless, but I don't feel it in me to make any changes for the better. A letter in the post cheers me up. I get an acceptance note for one of my poems in an upcoming anthology. It makes me feel good and motivates me to tidy up my recent literary work and submit it to publishers. When I write, I feel my life has purpose, but some days I am not capable of writing my name, let alone a poem. This good feeling dies quickly though, I just have to wait another day for rent and reality and bills to kill it. My existence is day to day but no life lived. I feel like I'm full of nothing left...

I wake up wanting to die as usual, but I'm too egotistical to be a corpse. I'm sure only half my mind belongs to me, and the other half I don't feel, don't know, or understand. I'm being tortured and tortured and tortured and not allowed to die. The life situation I find myself in is depressing; it makes me want to hurt myself. I don't really want to die but that's what it makes me feel like doing.

Someone told me to give up writing and find a realistic career. I told him to fuck off.

Withdrawing in disgust is not the same as apathy.

No thoughts turning in my mind, more like distorted images flashing momentarily and repeatedly: a heavy, dark sun, a pane of glass being shattered by a bullet, myself walking through an unfamiliar garden...

You could say I was a negative person...

I felt these appointments were pointless; that they consisted of me saying I wanted to die, and someone else writing about it. Usually I spoke in a monotone. My speech was so flat you could have done your ironing on it. My illness was as regular as clockwork; the pattern was the same: I'd have about 10 days of feeling okay, a few days of hypomania or mania, then 10 days of feeling shit, and then a couple of days of psychotic symptoms. I jealously guarded my periods of euphoria. I knew mental health professionals would construe it as mania. I didn't tell them about it because I didn't want them to break my high. Sitting in waiting rooms was enough to bring me down anyway. Like I said in one of my poems: I have accepted death sitting in waiting rooms.

I told Chris I just wanted to be alone and left alone. But then again I gave him the opposite message by turning up to every appointment so I would have a sounding board. Any interaction with my family always triggered suicidal ruminations or thoughts of non-lethal self-harm. I definitely felt I was being pushed around by my family but had little energy or motivation to assert myself. Chris suggested I go to an assertiveness training class, but ironically I was too scared of criticism to go.

Chris wrote: 'talked through her ideas of self-harm but Dolly isn't specific about the process.' Basically I saw it as an equation: pain + pain + suicide = no pain.

When you're severely depressed you think the world talks a load of old bollocks. So I listened to no one, least of all myself. I merely gave a platform to my inner demons, complete with an auditory hallucination orchestra. I begged many times to doctors and nurses to move me out of London, away from my family, but they said they couldn't do much about that. But they said they could help me manage my problems. I wanted to scream but couldn't be arsed to open my mouth. Tell me this shit, I thought privately, when you have my Dad living in the same house as you. You could say I was angry with them. They had no problem mucking about my brain chemistry but ensuring I had a safe and healthy place to live was not deemed necessary.

Chris tried to get me to talk about the past. I said: "There's no use crying over spilt milk." But I only needed a few more nudges from Chris, and I did cry over spilt milk, blood and tears that threatened to drown me. Chris challenged me not to 'universalise' my experience by thinking everything I do becomes bad and hopeless. But a shitty flat, a broken TV and an alcoholic father *was* my universe. When I wasn't depressed, I was noted as being frustrated, angry and hostile. Looking back I can see why. I am a hyper-creative person by nature, and at that time I was given no time, opportunity, tools and safe environment to be creative. All that excess energy had to go somewhere; I felt as if I was in a straitjacket 10 sizes too small. The only words I wanted to say to the world were: "FUCK YOU!

FUCK YOU! FUCK YOU ALL!" I said this to everyone I felt let me down, to those that didn't know me, and to those who helped me. I so mixed up, I wanted to rip open my skin and leave my body. I daydreamed about getting a gun and shooting up some people at the local town hall, at my old school, Safeways, I wasn't picky. I disclosed these violent imaginings to no one.

After 8 sessions, Chris discharged me from Lewin Road. He felt I was no longer presenting biological symptoms of depression. I thought: here we go, another person who said they were going to help, but would only do so for a little while, and then bugger off. I cursed Chris and the rest of the world. Psychosis and depression seemed to be much more faithful friends.

The year dragged on. I tried to sleep through the rest of it. During this time I had persistent fantasies of gouging out my eyes. I had seen enough of the world. A couple of times I would put a razor between my eye and the mirror. It didn't go further than that. Instead I carved razor smiles onto my skin. 'Look, I'm happy, you fuckers.' I'd think.

18 months after I last saw Chris, I was back at Lewin Road, yet another crisis referral. The voices had come back with full force. There were only a few times during the day when they were silent. Imagine being told of your own slow torture by gross demonic voices 24 hours a day. They told me not to tell anybody about them. When I did tell my GP, they said they were going to eat me whilst I was

asleep. I actually heard chewing noises and flesh being ripped apart. This never failed to shock me awake, and I would feel over my body for bite marks. Sometimes I experienced the physical pain of having teeth dig into my flesh. "Smile." Some stranger on the street would say to me. Can you understand why I wanted to kill the bastard?

I took an overdose of about 20 Prozac tablets. I had the shakes and sweated a lot but no sleep, let alone death. I told Chris I didn't want to die really, I just wanted to stop feeling they way I did. Imagine having your father repeat: "You fucking cunt!" a thousand times a day for a thousand days. Whilst I was cleaning out a bedroom I came across my old chemistry set. As per usual, Dad was snoring away on the sofa, with half a can of Tennents beside him. Voices told me to put all my leftover chemicals into his can of lager. I did this and watched over him and waited for him to die, but soon got bored and watched TV instead. I was not even guilty of attempted murder; all I gave him was indigestion. The voices laughed at my failure.

I felt utterly helpless, which is a common feature of depression. I can think of one incident with demonstrated this. I was in the kitchen watching TV. In the sink the tap was dripping, making that annoying 'plip-plop' sound. The irritation this engendered in me was as caustic as sulphuric acid. The dripping tap brought me to tears and almost drove me to the point of suicide. All I had to do was get up and shut the faucet off properly. When you are depressed your view of the world is so blank and dark, you just don't think of this. Depression paralyses you and blames you for the paralysis. I thought I deserved to die because of that dripping tap.

Some say people experiencing psychosis shouldn't undertake psychotherapy. In my case they were right. Chris and I were coming from two different worlds. I was definitely not of planet earth. I liked talking to Chris; it did sometimes alleviate the stress. But deeper, darker things were rumbling.

In 1999, there were periods of lucidity and normality, but the voices got so bad, I was seriously planning either suicide or murder just to shut them up; they teased and tormented me horrifically. I was so desperate I told Chris about them, even though the voices threatened world destruction if I did. Chris asked me what they said. I told him the voices said my father was planning to kill me and that I should kill him first. We discussed how distressing this was for me. I said I wanted to kill myself because they just wouldn't leave me alone.

By mid-March everything was falling apart. I wanted to die, but the voices said even in death they would be with me, and I believed them. "You're shit. Die, you bitch. Your family want you dead. They are planning your death right now." They tormented. When I sat with my family I believed they were giving each other signals concerning how to kill me. They could mind read and consequently were interfering with my thoughts. I was convinced they were aerials for demonic aliens. My delusion encompassed the whole world. I believed the world leaders were the puppets of an alien race that saw the destruction of the world as entertainment. The only writing I did in this period was about this. I wrote a booklet I wanted to distribute to the entire world, warning them and providing 'proof' of a forthcoming alien invasion. I found proof in the secret message from the TV news. I scoured the bible for references that would back me up. I opened the booklet with a quote from the Bhagavad Gita: "Brighter than a thousand suns radiated the glory of the deity, I see how you devour all mankind from all directions with your flaming mouths. With your shining glory you penetrate the whole universe... The deity spoke: 'There am I, the great shatterer of worlds, and I come to exterminate all mankind...' This, to me, was proof that UFOs were going to destroy humanity.

I wrote: 'God and demons are 2 splinter groups of the same alien race. The God aliens saw earth and wanted to conduct experiments and create a new life from. By infusion of their genetics to facilitate the process, homo sapiens came from monkeys.'

I also wrote: 'Reality is the greatest brainwashing technique ever successfully utilised and maintained. It makes the truth ludicrous and highly inconvenient to believe. But now I have been shown a small piece of the truth, I will discard this evil reality. Human beings are so self-centred. They have big discussions utilising tiny intellects, and assume they are the highest form of life. Probably cockroaches jabber on about how superior they are – that is until something bigger than them comes from above to squash them. Reality is living under false pretences. To control people's actions you need to control their thoughts. Demonic aliens do this by utilising psychic terrorism. They are trying to bring about an apocalypse, by inserting ideas and concepts and instructions into certain people, who will cause great destruction and disharmony, destabilising humanity...'

I also wrote about my family: 'Now they have taken over my family because they know I know about them and what they are trying to do. My 'family' don't look real any more; they are taken over by extraterrestrial impostors. They can read my thoughts, which is fucking scary and making me want to hit out. This is what they want, so they can call the police and get me out of the picture kitchen. So I'm stuck in the middle of a riddle.'

My sister Paula said something to me, I don't even remember what any more, and I tried to stab her with a pen. Thankfully I was unsuccessful, but I turned the pen on myself and then tried to climb out of the 3rd floor window. My Mum was screaming and crying, trying to pull me back in.

My next session with Chris, he asked me how I was. I said I felt better. Why was this? He asked. Because not only did my family want me dead, but so did my neighbours. When he challenged this perception, I got surly and told him maybe I'd better leave. I just had enough. Talking therapy and probably the whole book of psychiatric drugs had gone through my system, and I was still a few centimetres away from murder or suicide. Even though I was trying to focus on positive things in my life, the psychosis never went away. For example, I moved to a nice flat on a quiet road, which had a lovely garden out back, and was overjoyed. Concentrating on moving helped but only for short periods of time.

There is an argument about how to treat severe mental distress, whether to concentrate on the pharmacological side of it, or see the illness due to social factors like unemployment, domestic violence or bad housing. I think both are important influences. In the end, I needed the positive aspects of both. But it is important to give the person suffering the distress a choice about medication. I remember being given Stelazine and as a result of its sedative qualities, I could barely keep my eyes open. My psychiatrist pointed out my psychotic symptoms diminished under Stelazine, but did he really expect me to live the rest of my life as a zombie? The medication got rid of my psychotic symptoms – and my life too. We are more than just psychiatric symptoms and labels. Anti-psychotic drugs don't give you a meaning to life. They just calm you down enough to make it slightly easier to find one.

I was happy in my new home as a person who thought aliens were taking over could be. I spoke to a new neighbour. He told me the old woman who lived in my home before me died there. He was only making conversation but that flipped me out. I worried her spirit was still there. The voices I heard stopped talking: now they were screaming. Occasionally they quieted down and taunted me to stop them screaming. I was living in a world of unreal ultra-reality. "Who are you? Why are you doing this?" I begged of them. "Ask your Daddy. You're Daddy's girl, after all."

Hell raged inside my skull. Dad provided the externals. My Dad gave a face to the evil voices. I thought if he died, the screaming would stop. Just before a session with Chris, I stopped off at a pound shop and bought a carving knife; I became preoccupied with thoughts of stabbing my father as he slept. I believed I was telepathic, and saw that he was planning to burn the house down. I told Chris this; I told him my father had to die. "What do you think will happen to you if you did that?" He asked. "Oh, I'd go to jail, but my family and the world would be safe. "You'll end up in Broadmoor." He countered.

"Can I have a look at the knife, Dolly?" I showed it to him. He examined it. "Can I keep it for a few minutes?" He excused himself and left the room. I twiddled my thumbs.

He came back without the knife and with a psychiatrist. "I think you should go into hospital for a few days." The doctor said. "You're feeling pretty chaotic now, aren't you?"

I nodded.

"A stay in hospital will provide an oasis of calm for you. It'll be like a holiday." She said.

I agreed and phone calls were made. A bed was found for me at the Luther King ward at Southwestern Hospital (now Lambeth Hospital). Chris said he would drive me up there. First, I had to phone home to tell my family I was going into hospital. Sheila picked the phone up and I told her I was being admitted into hospital for depression. My poor sister began to get upset. "What's wrong, Dolly? What happened?" I couldn't tell her. I asked her to bring some clothes and toiletries in.

The car journey there was silent for the most part. For some reason I don't recall we began to talk about teachers. Chris said he thought I would make a good teacher once I was better and gained some confidence. I was touched by his warmth even though I was on a different planet to him.

I had no idea what to expect when I reached the psych ward. It wasn't full of strange-acting people, except maybe for some of the staff. It had an air of clinical monotony. Chris went into the ward office and the staff in there ignored both him and me. No one said hello or introduced him or herself. I knew they thought I was a knife-wielding maniac but a simple hello wouldn't go amiss. Chris spoke to a bored-looking agency nurse, who called a nursing assistant to show me where I was going to sleep. Because of nerves I already had the farts, so I was somewhat disappointed I had to sleep in a four-bed ward. I looked out of the window that overlooked the concrete garden of a different ward. One person was shuffling up and down it. I began to get a little bit tearful; I wanted to go home. A nursing assistant was called to show me around the ward. She showed me the laundry room, the games room with a snooker table in it, the ladies' TV room, the smoking room, the dining area, and the main TV room, and then she left me. I sat alone in the TV room. What treatment was I going to get, I remember thinking. A nurse called me and I was interviewed by a doctor about how I was feeling. I was already thinking ahead about how to get out of there. When the interview was over, my Mum, sister Sheila and Dawn, my Mum's friend, were waiting for me. My Mum ran up to me and hugged me. My thoughts about them being evil aliens suddenly seemed silly. "Why are you here?" My Mum asked me. "I want to die." I told her. She began to get tearful. "I just need time away from Dad." I said honestly. My Mum and my sister needed no further explanation. They realised they could end up on the ward because of Dad. They left and promised to visit me every day.

As it turned out, for the rest of my 6-week stay, I didn't see much of the nurses, usually only at the morning and evening medication calls. During my first stay in hospital no nurse sat me down and really talked about what would help me. If we passed in the corridor, they'd ask me how I was. My automatic response was, "I'm fine," They took me for my word, maybe because it saves them time. It's no surprise to anyone who has stayed on an acute psychiatric ward, that you get most of your compassion and therapy from your fellow patients. One time sitting in the TV room, I got quite tearful.

A black woman left the room and came back with a can of cola she had, opened it and gave it to me.

One thing that struck me when I finally read my notes. 'Calm and compliant with medication' was repeated too many times. Yes, on the outside I was as calm as catatonia, as quiet as death, only occasionally seen to be preoccupied with voices. My upbringing trained me to be blank and passive on the face of it. Inside, I was watching an insular apocalypse. Another thing that puzzled me when I obtained my psychiatric notes to help me write this book, was how they kept changing my ethnic background. By turns, I was Caucasian, Indian, and Anglo-Indian. And the last time I looked, psychosis doesn't shrink you. I'm 5'8", but on a physical observations page I became 5 foot 3. Of course there were nurses who were compassionate and empathic, but I got the distinct feeling the only 'care' patients were promised came out of a bottle of pills or a depot injection, to make us passive enough not to be too feeling; that was just too inconvenient for the health service and society in general.

My time on the ward was for most part a blur; it didn't seem real; I didn't feel real. I kept to myself for the most part, but sometimes I did go to the most popular part of the ward – the smoking room – for a chat with someone. The smoking room was at the far end of the corridor. The walls were stained yellow by nicotine, and cigarettes burns decorated the fake leather chairs. The cigarette burns didn't stop there. A few of its human occupants wore them too.

I remember being hypnotised by a Pakistani guy who compulsively ran his hand through his hair. Another person told me a refugee had been on the ward recently, who had been tortured in her home country. She hated her stay in hospital so much, she asked to be sent back to her country! It wasn't that bad for me, but that was because I was an informal patient and could leave the ward, and after a few days on the ward, I didn't expect to be helped or cured.   After about a week I was thoroughly bored. I tried to study for an OU course, but my concentration was shot, so I mostly doodled in my notebook. There was nothing to do but drink tea, watch TV, have your meals, and watch people get more and more distressed. I was pestered by a couple of guys on the ward who wanted me to go out with them or give them a blowjob. In fact, I got more attention from them than the nurses. I was utterly vulnerable but managed to tell them to fuck off. I knew a few of the women on the ward had been, as I had, sexually abused at one point in their lives. Being on a mixed ward therefore offered a spurious brand of therapy. Screaming patients were my 'oasis of calm'. The only useful thing I learnt was relaxation techniques in the movement group. I started spending time off the ward. I didn't go to my family or my own place, but instead took long walks. On one of these occasions there were delays on the train so I came back to the ward later than expected. A nurse scolded me as if I were a little child. Another time they were about to report me as AWOL when I was in fact back on the ward after a day trip. "Why didn't you tell anyone you were

133

back?" A nurse asked, which I thought was a stupid question, because I needed someone in the nurses' office to let me into the locked ward when I returned from my outing.

During my hospital stay I was on Olanzapine, the anti-psychotic, and gained two stone on it. Because I already had problems with my weight as I tended to comfort eat, I felt like a sumo wrestler. My psychiatrist talked more about my weight than the pain I felt.

Ward rounds meant going into a room full of people I didn't know to talk about my innermost feelings and thoughts. Was I a freak on show, a freak show that exposed the house of my soul – with ugly, dark, lonely rooms of anguished reminisces that mean absolutely nothing to anybody else. There was a definite sense of being outnumbered and outvoted. I wanted out of the fucking ward, so I lied, which was a shame because I did want help out of my personal hell, they just seemed to be adding to it. I continued to see Chris though. I told him how I really felt because I trusted him. So there was a discrepancy in what I told him and what I said to the staff on the ward. I saw him more as a human than a psychiatric nurse, that's why. I told him aliens were controlling us, taking over people in prominent positions, like the queen. I was pretty unshakable in these beliefs. I was convinced that it went all the way back to when I worked on 'The Empire Strikes Back'. It wasn't a fucking film, it was reality, and it was up to me to maintain the good and evil in the universe. But apart from that, I was just your average person in the street, a street I shared with demons and angels.

After 6 weeks on the ward, I was discharged. I was glad to be out. At first my family didn't know what to say to me, but Kenny cracked a few jokes to break the ice, and I began to talk about my hospital stay. They were all supportive, all except my Dad. He wasted no chance to call me crazy. Even when he had shit in his pants, he thought he was superior to me because he was not crazy.

When I was in hospital I talked to a social worker a couple of times, and asked her to help me with my housing benefit claim, as I was getting letters threatening eviction. This caused a lot of stress for me. She said she would sort it out, but back into the wonderful world of the community, the letters kept coming, and it was easy to slip into a heavy depression again. As far as I can see it, society/bureaucracy, whatever you want to call it, contributes to the depression of the individual. Anyone who has been to a dole or housing benefit office will bear this out. The 'service' from the people on the other side of the desk is resentful or patronising. If you are already vulnerable because of your precarious mental state and go to these places, you get ripped apart. And nobody cares. Your doctor doesn't want to hear about it. Your psychiatrist doesn't want to hear about it, your social worker doesn't want to hear about it.

I have no doubt these bureaucratic, self-arse-licking organisms have contributed to people's suicides, or worsened their mental illness. And do they care that they do this? No, they probably see it as one less case to worry about. I would like to find out about those in Lambeth who had a mental illness and subsequently committed suicide, how many of them had problems with benefits, housing, etc. What is it with bureaucratic establishments' obsession to break your spirit? I didn't know the human soul was so troublesome to those in charge of the paperwork. After several soul-destroying visits to housing and benefit offices, I managed to sort out the mess, and it was back to the pain of ordinary life.

I spent time at my new flat, doing it up or sitting in the cold garden. There were periods of hypomania. There was a pain just under my shoulder blades and I was convinced this was because someone ripped off my angelic wings while I was asleep. I saw the god essence in lollipop ladies. I hugged old ladies at bus stops because they looked lonely; every single one of them thought I was after their purses. I made plans to free the animals at London Zoo. On the day of their planned release I took a tube into Central London, but because of my high and chaotic mental state, I got lost. So I walked around instead, laughing at people's thoughts. I also made plans for a utopian society while my family was falling apart.

Our first concrete attempts to stand up to our Dad were met with unoriginal violence. When he saw that didn't faze us, he burst into tears. "Don't you love me? You would do as I say if you loved me. Don't be cruel to me." I was gob smacked and said, "By not letting you abuse us any more, we're being cruel to you?" He thought about this for one minute and said, "Yes." I was so disgusted I had to leave the room. I went into the kitchen to drink some water and calm down. A few minutes later Sheila came in tearfully. "What's a matter?" I asked her. "Dad said he has stomach cancer. That's why he's been going to the hospital." "Are you sure?" I asked. She nodded.

I went straight to my father and asked him if it was true. He gave me a wink. "No, I only said that to make Sheila feel bad for deserting me."

"You shouldn't say things like that to people!" I screamed at him. How can you reach a person like that? I'm well aware certain mental health professionals were thinking the same thing about me.

Taking a step back, I saw my father was stuck in a vicious circle that was rolling further and further downhill. He was unable to maintain sobriety because that meant he'd have to think about all the awful things he did while he was drunk. All his memories were regretted. So it was always back to the drink to block these memories out and create abysmal new ones. I would sometimes watch my father sit in his seat, oozing sickness, hate and pain. How much pain can a 67 year old body absorb? And why did he have to wear it all in the eyes, those eyes that stared hard at me?

Christmas 1999 was a good laugh – when Dad wasn't around. It was his yearly tradition to cry for his dead mother on Christmas Day. And because he was upset he had to go out and get drunk. When he came back in the evening, he flopped out on his bed, wet his pants, and shouted at us to keep quiet.

The year 2000 came and most of the world celebrated. To me it was a bunch of numbers at the end of some celestial utility bill. The year 2000 had been significant for me in my delusions. It meant the beginning of the end. Aliens would use the new millennium to do their worst. I wrote in my notebook: 'Aliens influence history. The star of Bethlehem is a UFO. Influence. Influence. Influence. Our planet to them is just a hopelessly dumb animal that needs to be put out of its misery. The year 2000 is its sacrificial altar...' This disheartened me. The shade of black has no problem getting darker. Depression turned my body, mind and soul into concrete; procrastination turned my heart into a block of dirty ice. Dying was too much like hard work; living was too much like hard work. The orchestra of nihilism became my auditory hallucinations again. At this time my Mum's bathroom was leaking water into the flat below. Plumbers came and went without fixing the problem. I decided they were not plumbers but spies sent to check up on me. I thought the phone was bugged. Because I knew of the aliens' existence, they were persecuting me. By the end of January I was back in hospital again.

There were some old faces of people who were in the last time I was there. There was one guy who, when I was in there last, liked to crawl through the serving hatch in the dining room and scare the catering staff. When I returned to the ward for the second time, he had turned into the TV room sage, wise and silent, offering sensible advice. What is he on, I wondered. I was glad, this time round, to be offered my own room, even if they didn't bother to provide clean sheets; I went back out into the corridor and bumped into a nurse. I told him my bed sheets needed changing. He apologised and cleared up the dirty linen immediately.

Among the new faces on the ward was a guy who liked to wear all of his clothes at once until he could barely walk. He also liked to build forts in the TV by turning a sofa upside down. On returning to the ward after a day out he would bring things he found on the street, like a broken typewriter or half a hat. When he found out I was reading Kerouac, he begged to read the book after me. I let him have my copy. For the most part I hid out in my room, reading the graffiti on the wall. Jesus was in the room one time. Talking to people was too much hard work. I only spoke to people at medication times or in the meal queue. That was all I could take at the time. The food wasn't too bad, a bit bland. One dinner queue inspired a poem:

Q

Dinner queue in the psych ward
I'm stuck between 2 Jesuses
I can see they're both contemplating
feeding the 5 thousand by doing a
miracle of multiplication with the
rubbery macaroni cheese
A schizophrenic soul abuses
any god that is listening
The catatonic philosophises
with empty words
The anorexic looks down her
nose at us for indulging in
the depravity of sustenance
Why am *I* here?
Reality, sanity is a book of
lies, I've lost my page
I've become celestially illiterate
Because I know the ending – no
happily ever after
just lonely death
following
a life
that is just a queue
waiting, waiting
for the
madness to end

They put me on Clozapine. There is a possibly fatal side effect to the drug, so you need to have your blood tested regularly, which I hated. The veins in my arms are too deep, so I'm hard to get blood out of. Sometimes it took three or four attempts. Again because of boredom and a sense of duty to my Mum, I spent more time off the ward than on. My Mum didn't like being alone at home with my Dad, so I felt guilty if I wasn't with her. This exasperated one of the nurses responsible for my care. She said, "You shouldn't be worried about who is looking after your Mum. At the moment, you're the one that needs looking after." But she wasn't patronising. I liked her. She took the time out to sit me down explain the effects of the new drug I was on. Once when I was distressed by voices during the night, she told me not to keep it to myself, but to tell the nightshift about it. She talked to me as an equal, which meant the world to me.

But even at my most depressed, I can't abide idle hands. The boredom was vitriolic. Because the blurred vision my new medication gave me, I was not even able to read or write. Either that or the psychic channel-hopping, which meant I went from one thought to the next too quickly, so that nothing made sense in my head. Just to get away from the ward, I went to Clubhouse one day a week, a work project for people with mental health difficulties, where I helped out with basic office duties. Another side effect I had endure was excess saliva. I'm a shy person anyway, so I found talking to other people even harder.

But the drug did the job. I was stabilised after three months and discharged. But medication is never the whole answer. If you leave hospital to return to a hellish environment, it's still hell. You're just made a little bit number as not to feel it. To paraphrase Freud, "Their job was to transform neurotic or psychotic misery into ordinary human unhappiness." I came out of hospital to a house of pain. The whole household was tense and desperate. Mum was in the process of evicting my father with the help of her social worker and solicitor. The look in my Dad's eyes shredded my soul into a thousand useless pieces. "Why doesn't anybody love me?" He would say. Then in the same breath, he would call us, "A bunch of fucking cunts."

The anti-psychotic medication I was given was unable to tranquillise that look in my father's eyes. Finally the day came and my father was officially evicted. He went to the local homeless person unit; they put him up in B&B. His memory was deteriorating at an alarming pace, and I was worried he wouldn't be able to cope on his own. Whenever I saw him he kept repeating the question, "What day is it?

I didn't know how to help him without hurting or undermining myself. The stress this was causing me made a joke of the medication I was taking. My inner demons became comedians, making fun of my confusion. In my vulnerable state I felt guilty about everything so I let my Dad stay at my Mum's for a while if he refrained from drinking. He spent his nights at the hotel, and the day at my Mum's. He was sober... at first. Then the drink came, the abuse followed, and the pain was at home with itself. I didn't know whether I hated or loved my father; whether I wanted him dead or alive.

But because I had been in hospital two times in six months and wasn't looking forward in returning there, I tried not to show my pain. My mother expected me to protect her from Dad all the time; this drained me. My Mum's dependence on me strung me out. What was frustrating she would ask for my opinion, but never, ever take it. My parents acted like two truculent kids. This is why hospitalisation is sometimes a waste. People get better in hospital and then return to the bad situation that facilitated the breakdown in the first place.

Would my life ever change?

PART THREE

'With certain creative people it's a do-or-die situation – to not commit suicide or homicide you must create..." Lydia Lunch

I had applied for the benefit Disability Living Allowance and was turned down. Some months later I went to a DLA appeal and they decided to award me the benefit. There were three women on the adjudication panel and they talked to me as an equal. I hope this means the benefits system is changing for the better. Probably not, though. I think I was lucky to get those three people. Some weeks later, the backdated money was placed in my account, just over £1000. I had never been in possession of that much money before. I paid off some bills and debts. I was too scared to spend the rest of the money so I left it for a while to gather dust and interest.

My Mum had a pile of holiday brochures she didn't need any more. I had a quick glance through a few of them. One American coach holiday caught my eye, with stops at places I dreamed of visiting, such as the Grand Canyon. I had never been to a travel agent before and a bit daunted about going to one, but I took a deep breath and aimed straight there to book it. The lady behind the desk was very helpful, explaining anything I didn't understand. Paying for it took a sizable chunk of my money, but I thought: this is what it is for – to enjoy life, not to keep under mattress until you're too old to spend or enjoy it.

The day before the flight, I couldn't sleep because of the anticipation. My Mum had told me horror stories about ears popping on flights. So when the plane was ready to finally take off, I gripped the headrest in front of me and clenched my teeth. But I needn't have bothered; the flight was great and I found out I loved flying. Even though serious turbulence I had great fun.

I landed in LA and the holiday rep met me and put me on bus for the hotel. We were told to eat and rest and the coach holiday would start the next day. Using a key card and traveller's checks for the first time made me realise how much I pulled myself away from the ordinary world, and doing these simple things made me feel less of an alien.

The first two days of the holiday were spent in Disneyland and Universal Studios, childhood fantasises fulfilled in adulthood. I don't mind admitting I laughed and squealed like a child at the many attractions. Although I had an interest in Buddhism, I had never met a Buddhist monk or nun. But I met some in the most unlikely of places. At the Waterworld attraction full pyrotechnics, stunts, and yes, lots of water, a group of Buddhist monks took up an entire bench to watch the show. The compere squirted water at them. Instead of being angry they laughed until I thought they were going to fall out of their robes. When the show was over I went to talk to them and the head monk explained some points on Buddhism I didn't understand. After our conversation, they went back into Waterworld for a second drenching!

The next day we left Los Angeles behind and headed south towards Mexico. The holiday rep Robin deviated from the script she was supposed to read and gave her own anecdotes, which were fair more interesting, stories about her strict Mormon mother and her fireman hubby. Most of the other passengers were retired couples, and as I was the youngest person on the coach, they spoilt me rotten. They made sure I had enough sunscreen on, they bought me lunches and ice creams and little gifts. I loved it!

We stopped off at San Diego for a few hours. I had a coffee in Balboa park, brought a couple of tie-dyed t-shirts from a street vendor and had lunch of a vegetarian melt served up by a crew of Mexican teenagers.

Nearing the Mexican border, we had to exchange our luxury coach for a rattling, slightly the worse for wear, yellow school bus, which was going to take us across the border. The driver of the school bus stopped to let on a Mexican man with a guitar. He was going to provide the musical accompaniment for the border crossing. He played about 5 well-known Spanish songs, and made us sing along and clap to the music. His finale was "La la bamba! Pass the cup! La la bamba! Give me money!" He had lifted everybody's mood so he did very well, his tin cup teeming with dollars. Once in Tijuana I left the oldies and did a little shopping and downed a few tequilas with a group of crazy college kids who loved my London accent. They told me their trips to Tijuana were a regular excursion because of the cheap legal and illegal drugs available there. They asked me to stay with them for a couple of days but I had to rendezvous with the oldies.

Entering Mexico from the US was no problem and pretty quick. Trying to enter the US from Mexico took a little bit longer. The queue in front of us was at least 300m long, dotted with Mexican nationals who wanted to live in the US. Someone told me you see the same Mexican faces every day, they have nothing better to do, and who knows, one day they might be lucky. Finally the coach load of us managed to cross the border with no problems, and the coach took us to our hotel in San Diego.

The next day we travelled through the deserts of Arizona. It was naked, and sparse and haunting, the heat undeniable. I saw my first giant cacti, I felt like I was in a cowboy movie. We had our lunch at a diner that stood alone in the desert. The beauty of the dusty earth took my breath away and came back with my soul. Our hotel was in Scottsdale, where a meat barbeque was on offer. Being a vegetarian I declined, and chose to go for a walk. Arizona seemed to be really into their meat because the only places open at night was McDonalds and a few steakhouses. I went into the McDonalds for a cold drink. Behind the McDonalds you could see the desert. It was amazing. How could I feel bad about life when there are things like that? Back at the hotel, I watched a little TV before going to sleep. People in the UK usually moan there are too many American TV programmes on the box. In the US, it was the opposite: there was nothing but British TV, such as Keeping Up Appearances, Robot Wars, and Antiques Roadshow.

From Phoenix we travelled north and left the low desert behind. We reached Sedona in mid morning. It's a New Age town situated at the bottom of Oak Creek Canyon, where people threatened to cleanse my aura. Of course they charged for it, so I declined. This great holiday was doing a perfectly good job cleaning out my soul. Finally we made it to the place that was my reason for taking the holiday: the Grand Canyon. I wasn't disappointed. The magnitude of its beauty brought tears to my eyes. There was no doubt it was bigger than any human being, greater than any god. The changing sun transformed the colours of the rock and brought them alive. It may be just a tourist attraction for some, but for me it was a changing point in my life: I could no longer completely believe in suicide any more, not when life could give me this. I was one step from the edge of the cliff, and the stunning view stopped me in my tracks; I was unable to take another step. I took a 7-mile hike in the Grand Canyon, where I saw a deer and a baby snake. When I returned to the coach I found a small lizard in my bag. I let the little bugger go.

The next day we travelled along the south rim of the Grand Canyon to our first stop the Navajo

Nation, an Indian Reservation. A Native American gave us a tour in a ragged school bus that had no glass in the windows. Red dust blew into our eyes and faces. We were all given wet wipes at the end and we needed them, we were so dusty. There was even a souvenir stall, selling Native American goods. I felt uncomfortable capitalism made its encroachment here, but if you're an ordinary guy who wants to feed his family, what choice do you really have?

We drive through Monument Valley where the sun played on exquisite rock formations. Again, I felt like I was in a cowboy movie, and we were told a lot of the early cowboy films were filmed there. We stopped off at Page for the night.

The next day the coach took the long drive to Las Vegas, passing Bryce Canyon and Zion National Park to get there. Just sitting back and watching the landscape ease away was hypnotic. I said to myself I could spend the rest of my life like this, no problem. It was evening when we reached Las Vegas. I stayed at the Circus Circus hotel, which had a roller coaster ride inside the building. The night was ours to spend. I just wandered about town, getting sucked into the quicksand of neon. I think I was the only person in town who didn't gamble. I much preferred to people-watch. I caught a couple of shows, one of a mutiny on a pirate ship with lots of explosions and stunts; the other was a musical performed by hippies on stilts. I also witnessed a wedding at a 24-hour chapel from a distance. The night was hot. The day had been 119° so I didn't really wander far from the hotel. When I hit the sack it was already the next day.

We passed through Death Valley for lunch, I don't remember much about it. Maybe only my death was making notes. It was back to LA again, where I caught a train up to San Francisco. I spent the last 3 days of my holiday in the city and absolutely loved it. I had that distinct feeling I had been there before, definitely in a former life. I didn't even need a map for chrissakes. I took a tram ride to Fisherman's Wharf and then visited Alcatraz. I visited Golden Gate Park and the City Lights Bookstore. The next day, just after the sun rose, I went for a walk in the dawn city. I ambled over to Washington Square and watched some oldies do Tai chi. They saw me sitting there watching and invited me to join them. I shyly accepted and had a free tai chi lesson. The previous day I booked a place on a bus tour of the city. The driver/guide was a poet, and amidst his commentary, he told us anecdotes. He was so interesting that I sometimes forget to pay attention to the city outside my window. He had a pile of his books on the dashboard for sale and I bought one, which I read on the plane home. Undoubtedly this trip was one of the best experiences of my life.

Chris saw the positive impact the trip had on me. I told him I wished I were back on my trip. He said that was common, that travelling provides peak experiences the ordinary day-to-day humdrum life can't compete with. But it wasn't only that. I was back in the same country, same city, and same town as my father. He didn't magically disappear. A couple of weeks back from my holiday and Dad came to the flat drunkenly violent, demanding to be let in. Only Mum was home and she watched him charge continuously at the door with his shoulder. The dogs were hiding under the furniture. Mum was so scared she dialled 999 and kept repeating the word 'help' down the phone, hoping the police would trace the call. They did and came to the flat at the same time as Paula. The police warned my Dad off and took the keys to the flat he still had on him.

Sheila's wedding was approaching and I dreaded to think what Dad would do to spoil it. I told Sheila, quite unfairly, that if she invited Dad to the wedding, I wouldn't go. As it turned out, he wasn't fit or sober enough to attend. Kenny gave away Sheila, and the ceremony went well, except for the organist's drunken rendition of The Wedding March. It was nice day; I felt like a normal person who did the things ordinary people did. It made for a beautiful summer; I felt great. But the expansive feeling soon went as mania took over. My energy was large enough to fill the Grand Canyon. I revisited America in my dreams and woke up convinced I did really go there. One night I dreamt my sister Sheila died. I spent the morning crying, believing she was dead. When she rang about midday, I thought I had a telephone connection with heaven. I asked for the number. My excessive energy resided in a body far too small, in a mind that was far too big. Electricity crackled and cackled in my bones. Power surges explode appliances – I knew the feeling. My body was a straitjacket I needed to get out of. I was incapable of sleeping. I spent the whole night dreaming, planning, and creating. I came up with something that would save the world. Instead of using fossil fuels, I came up with an invention that turned noise into energy. It was just a shame I forgot the important details and schematics when I got up. The day lasts longer for a manic. I believed I could write a novel in a day. I was convinced of my telekinetic powers. I spent the whole day in an armchair, staring at a ball, willing it to move. The chaos theory originated in my mind. Butterflies flapping their wings in China cause hurricanes in Hawaii, and my mind was creating a million butterflies a second. I was convinced I was able to change the world through thought. "I have to stay positive," I kept repeating to myself. And when I didn't have a positive thought I slapped my own face. I also thought I was living one day ahead of everybody else. I was in Wednesday while everyone else was still in Tuesday. I was fading in and out of worlds, in and out of death, the animal realm, the hungry ghost realm, heaven, hell. I was remembering my divinity in supermarket aisles. Mania became a state of compulsive epiphany.

While all this was happening, my father's condition was deteriorating. The police picked him up a few times in a disorientated state and took him up to St Thomas' Hospital; but father always discharged himself when he sobered up. He sat on a bench in the green in front of Brixton Library – a favourite hang out for drunks and druggies. Other substance abusers stole his money, his glasses and his walking stick when he was too drunk to resist. I found him once sleeping on the streets. Sometimes he went missing for days without any idea where he'd been. Needless to say, this was adversely affecting my mental state.

Yet again I became obsessed with my father's death. Browsing a bookstore in Croydon, I came across a spell book. I was *meant* to find that book, I thought to myself. There was one spell which purported to get ride of the people causing you pain. I followed the ritual to the letter and waited, and waited, and waited. Nothing happened. Flies swarmed around him but he wasn't dead yet. If you walked past him, the smell of him would make you want to gag. With psychiatric professionals that was all I could talk about. They all said the same thing: "You're next stop is Broadmoor." Reading the notes of the time, Chris raises the possibility of seeking a forensic opinion. Sectioning me was in the air. Other diagnoses were thrown in, such as borderline personality.

"You've got your Daddy's eyes and your Daddy's lies. Cut them out!" I was taking dictation from my psychosis again.

I'm standing over my sleeping father with a knife in my hand. Because he is a demonic alien plotting my destruction, he has to die; I am going to bring down the knife down on his face. "Look who's laughing now," I say. It doesn't matter to me that I am heading for a special hospital or eventual suicide. It didn't matter because I did what I had to do to survive. Can't people understand that?

As he sleeps, I watch him, waiting for the right moment to kill. Waiting. Waiting. His awful body odour, the old food in his beard, the spit marks on the floor, just makes me angrier and angrier. I raise the knife, ready to plunge it into this fucking waste of a human being. Another set of eyes is staring at me, from the wall. It is a picture of me as a child, smiling for the camera. I try 3 times to stab my father's skull, but a child is watching, and I can't do it. "I'm sorry for turning you into a murderer," I say to the photo. "I used to be a child once, I used to be a little girl..."

Something happened, something clicked. I couldn't let that child live this kind of life. Suddenly my Dad sobs in his sleep. I can't do it. I can't hurt him more than he's hurt himself. And he can't hurt me more than I've hurt myself. It has to stop. It has to stop *now*.

Now that suicide and homicide was no longer a lifestyle choice I was at a loss as to what to do. I decided the first thing to sort out was help for my father. I asked social services for help. They said they couldn't help without a medical referral. I took my father back to the GP surgery, this time seeing another doctor, one who I knew would have more empathy. She wasn't my father's usual doctor but she saw straight away my father's inability to look after himself: he stank, he was dishevelled, and kept asking the same question. She tested his memory with a few simple questions and he failed abysmally. She referred him to the Maudsley Hospital.

Chris, my key worker, saw how all this was adversely affecting me and also wrote to the hospital, supporting my case that I wasn't up to being his carer and that he did need care.

Some weeks later he eventually did see a psychiatrist who spent most of her interview testing his memory; he also had a few blood tests. They said he wasn't ill enough to be sectioned. Instead they arranged for him to see a CPN regularly and to attend the Felix Post Unit, a day centre in the hospital. His psychiatrist also arranged for social services to provide a home help, which they did. The problem he was hardly ever at his flat to let the CPN or home help in; he would go wandering and then forget where he lived. The only good thing was at least at the Felix Post he'd have a meal.

But the drinking would not subside. He let winos into his flat to sleep, a couple of which were really frightening in their drunken behaviour, so I went my father's flat less and less. When I did see him we would always clash verbally, arguing which one of us was the craziest. I said he was but it was clear I was riding the downward spiral into psychosis and paranoia again. I began to think aliens were controlling my father's behaviour to thwart my discovery of their worldwide network. This is what I wrote on a scrap of paper around about this time: *What is the devil? What is its form? How does he operate? What is his influence? Is he God's enemy? God's brother? Or God himself? The evil electricity of his power won't let me think my own thoughts. His telephone rays shine into my hopeless dogma mind. How am I supposed to function when my being is used as a psychic puppet? Lampshade camel sunrise on this morning of prickly slumber doom guard sunlit hopeful. Can the pain in my eye see its own dark colour? Cold sunburn. Hell is a quiet, lonely thing. There's nobody else there. So lonely, you wish for the presence of the devil...*

I may have resolved not to kill him but the anger was trying its best to hang on. Once when Dad came to Mum's place while I was there, I grabbed him by the scruff of neck and pushed him down the stairs. He came back the next day without any memory of the previous day's incident. That was when I knew he wasn't putting on the dementia, and I was remorseful for being physically aggressive towards him. He became a pathetic, derelict irony. To be a good liar you need an excellent memory. A conman with dementia – what a joke. But who was laughing? Not that it mattered he was going senile, we stopped believing him long ago. He would say, "Give me a fiver. I owe Oscar money." Oscar had been dead for over a year. The new situation provided a poignancy that was hard to swallow, especially when he went off to see friends of his who were dead but he thought were alive. And those that were alive ignored him. Even his own children were crossing the road to avoid him. One time I looked out of the window and saw him sitting all by himself. That broke my heart, and I cried at this sorry sight. I wanted to invite him inside and let him tell me his jokes, but I knew it wouldn't end happily ever after. I knew he would revert back to being a megalomaniac with a heart of gold because he just didn't know how to be anything else. It's painful to see an old man still acting like a hurt little boy. What a waste of life. The longer he sat alone, the longer I cried. Him being an arsehole I understood, knew and expected. But when he sends me a card saying 'I love you'. *That* I can't handle. I wanted to get out of the world that had him in it. It was just too painful.

But now that Dad was gone my Mum became a different person. She more or less stopped acting like a child. Dad definitely infantilised all of us – and when we started acting like adults, I knew why: being in an adult world scared the shit out of my father. With the help of her deaf friend Dawn, she learnt to be more independent and not to rely on me too much. I didn't feel so pressurised now, yet my mental instability was on a razor-edge seesaw for months. High and low. High and low on a psychological bungee rope. One of the things about manic depression is that once you come out of it, you have to deal with a lot of painful consequences because of poor judgement. I guess the worst one I had to deal with an unwanted pregnancy and subsequent abortion.

Thanks to my severe depression I pretty much stayed asexual throughout my 20s. When my mental health returned so did my sex drive but I chose to be celibate because of the Buddhist vows I took. There was another reason: I am bisexual and deemed that this would complicate my already convoluted life.   I wanted to concentrate on my writing so I didn't seek any relationships out. But

157

with hypomania or mania, sex was all I could think about. When this happened I would phone my exs or pick up strangers.

November 4th 2000 I went to an organised firework display, and I was somewhat hyper. The display's beautiful colours and loud bangs made my heart beat a little faster and my mind go a little higher. I had a one night stand with a fellow spectator.

A few weeks later when my mind returned to base, I regretted that incident. In fact, it threw me into a horrible self-hating depression. On New Year's Day, I was nauseous, my breasts were tender, I was putting on weight, and I had a metal taste in my mouth. I didn't think I could be pregnant as I hardly had any periods in 2000 and we had used a condom. It was only when I came across a TV article about the early signs of pregnancy did I seriously entertain the thought I could be pregnant. On January 2nd I went to the chemist and purchased a pregnancy kit. I had to pee on a stick and wait a couple of minutes for the indicator to change colour or not. I didn't have to wait 2 minutes to know I was pregnant; the indicator changed colour almost instantly. I was in shock, my mind went blank, I couldn't believe it. On January 3rd I took another pregnancy test – positive again. I think I spent the whole of that day crying. What the hell was I going to do?

I kept it to myself until the next day when I confided in Chris I was pregnant. He asked me what I was going to do. I don't know, I told him.

"You have to come to a decision soon, Dolly."

"Is it possible any of the medication could adversely affect the foetus?" I asked.

"It's possible. Prozac is okay, but Quetiapine is a relatively new drug, we just don't know. Go home and think this thing through."

So I went to my Mum's home and ruminated about it. I had the flat to myself. My heart was telling me to keep it; my head countered, "Are you crazy!" As I was thinking about it, my dad rang the intercom bell downstairs. I didn't want to have to deal with him so I didn't answer it. The door must have been unlocked because he managed to get up the stairs to my Mum's front door. He rang the bell constantly for a solid 3 or 4 minutes, sending the dogs crazy, and me even crazier. "Please go away!" I mouthed.

He didn't. Instead he banged on the door, slurring drunkenly, "Let me in!"

"Shut up! Shut up!" I cried.

"LET ME FUCKING IN!"

I made my decision at that moment: I was going to have a termination. There was no way I was going to bring a baby into this environment. Everything pointed to not keeping it – I was living in a one bedroom flat that wasn't big enough for a baby as well. I could have applied for a 2-bedroom place but what if it was on the top floor of a tower block or on a dodgy estate? I was still clinically depressed and could see no way out of the darkness; I was in debt, and I was unable to bear the thought of bringing up a baby and having to deal with my Dad as well. You have to understand at that time nobody would help me with regards to him. I was also taking a new drug where the effects of a developing foetus were not known.

I told Chris of my decision. He said whatever you chose to do, we'll support you. You should tell your Mum, he also counselled.

"No, I can't. She doesn't believe in abortion."

"Why, is she Catholic?"

"No, but she had 5 kids by a violent man. Of course she doesn't believe in abortion."

I was not unconscious of the pro-life and pro-choice tug-of-war. I became very disillusioned with both sides. I felt they never really cared about the pregnant woman or her child, all they were concerned with was scoring points of each other and being judgemental. Where was the practical support for the pregnant woman if she wanted to keep the child but her environment made it very difficult or impossible? If you think social workers, housing officers, and the benefits agency are there to help, you are very naive. I felt like the pregnant woman was a pawn in the game these two sides played.

I vacillated between wanting to keep the baby and getting an abortion. I wanted to tell my Mum but I just couldn't. I kept it to myself, crying in hidden corners. My depression teetered on psychosis again; I began to think the foetus was possessed. Through my GP, I made an appointment at the abortion clinic. My Mum noticed I wasn't eating and that I was physically and mentally off. She stopped me one time and demanded to know what was wrong. I blurted out I was pregnant and that I was having the termination because I was certain the baby was brain-damaged because of my medication. She took me in her arms and hugged me. I cried with relief.

My Mum is a very maternal woman and she is always going on about grandchildren, but she stood by my decision and gave me unconditional love and support. She was marvellous; she saved me from the brink.

She went with me to the clinic on the day of the termination. It took a couple of hours and then we were ushered into the post-op room with the other women. Most of them were sobbing, a nurse cruelly said to one, "Haven't you finished crying yet?"

According to the literature of the clinic most women feel relief after their termination, and I did for the first few days. Then I felt the most awful guilt. What if the medication hadn't affected the foetus? What if my living circumstances changed for the better? What if… What if?

I couldn't get the thought out of my head that I had consigned my Mum's first grandchild into the bin. Auditory hallucinations of the dead foetus haunted me. Then my sister announced she was pregnant. The moment was bittersweet. I was happy for my sister but incredibly jealous she was going to get to keep hers. Unfortunately she miscarried. I thought this was my fault too, that I upset some cosmic plan because I got rid of mine. Those feelings almost triggered another heavy depression, but through meditation I was able to keep some perspective.

What do I feel about it now? I should have taken the risk and kept the baby. The things I worried about worked themselves out. My CPN Nadir told me it's easy to look back in hindsight, but at the time I made the right choice. My head believes this, but as for my heart, it's another story...

Chris left Lewin Road for a new job whilst I had my termination. When I needed him the most, he wasn't there to talk to. But that was cool in a way. It meant it was entirely up to me to face it and gave me the motivation to change my life. I was transferred from the Treatment & Assessment Team to the Case Management Team, which deals with those who have severe and enduring mental health problems. Chris's replacement was Nadir, a CPN. He was easy to talk to and had a kind heart, so that was a relief. I no longer wanted counselling at this point. What I needed was practical support in regards to my father to make sure he got the right help, etc.

I have to say the termination was the biggest turning point in my life. I obviously had to make some changes in life for the better. It matured me like nothing before it. I was no longer able to believe depression's self-indulgent bullshit. I saw the futility of self-pity. I could no longer blame the world around me. I had to take responsibility for my life. I needed to build up self-respect and throw away negativity. For many years I promised myself I would change...tomorrow. The abortion now filled my actions with a sense of urgency. No more fucking about. No more blaming my father for all my ills. No more procrastination. I came up with a little Buddhist prayer to help me along: '**Now** is the knowing. **Now** is the living. **Now** is the loving. **Now** is the giving.'

I began to meditate seriously. I saw my thoughts had no power except the power I gave them. Thoughts arose and then ceased; I no longer identified with them. I saw that it is easier to succeed than it is to fail. Being a failure is a lot of work - all that mental energy and soul investment into negativity. Low self-esteem's mantra is: 'I cannot do this' or 'I'm not worth it'. I was no longer going to let a sentence that doesn't even last 3 seconds dictate the whole of my life. I utilised the trick of looking upon each day as my last day of life, and filled it with good things. There was no more time to think up things to hurt or control other people; I saw the utter waste of that. I was going to go to sleep and to my eventual deathbed with a smile on my face. There was no doubt I needed to get a life, especially when my flat's previous dead resident got more Christmas cards than me! I was staggered at how self-centred the depression made me. The more you think about yourself, the more depressed you get. And because I considered myself to be intelligent, my thoughts about myself had to be right. But you can be an intellectual and be emotionally and empathically stunted, with half a soul. When I started to pull away from self-centredness, the happier I became. I signed up to do voluntary work with BookAid, an organisation that sends books to the poorer parts of the world; and with Crisis, the homeless charity. I also gave blood. I began to feel good about myself. I saw in life something more beautiful than TV watching, anger and hate. I threw myself into Buddhist practice. Meditation de-stressed me, made me a calmer person. I had more energy without it turning it into full-blown mania. I saw the senselessness in being judgemental. It doesn't help you or the person you're judging, so what's the fucking point? You feel a spurious flash of power, that's all.

I was certainly bitter and twisted. But I'm glad I finally woke up and realised what a bunch of bullshit that was. What a waste of life if you carry that attitude to your death. I will never go back to that way of thinking again. I don't doubt I will be ill again; I'm just no longer going to piss gasoline on the psychotic fire.

Which of course meant forgiving my father. That was the hardest thing to do. I wanted to hold onto the pain; I thought it made me what I am. I saw if I didn't forgive him, I was in effect handcuffing myself to the pain for life. If someone's handed you a piece of shit, it doesn't mean you have to carry it around for life. Letting go is an amazing feeling. But writing this book has helped me not to become complacent. There is still much pain to deal with, there are still tears, and there is still anger. I know I haven't forgiven my father 100%, but even 80% will improve your life one thousand fold. As I've got older and made my own mistakes, I saw I had no right to judge my parents. As The Smith's song goes: '[They] are human and need to be loved…'

I may no longer devote my life to suicidal or homicidal thoughts and actions, but there is still a lot of surplus and jagged energy to make use of.

There is a fire in me that the 9-5 rat race is too much of a pussy to handle. I think it's fair to say those who have had long-term mental health problems and then have a period of lucidity present itself, realise there are so many things they have missed out on. Moving from insanity to being well is moving from one world to another, and is pretty scary. I mean, what are you supposed to do with your life once you've stopped battling demons? It's very strange being sane and having the memories of a mad person. It is very much like a dreamlike state, and sometimes sanity touches my head like a razorblade pillow. I found I could hide behind my illness, escape from the world that scared me, bored me, and fucked me over. I wasn't expected to be part of society. In my apathy this was appreciated. It was only when I started to live again, I felt the eviscerating rejection of society, the understanding that I had no worth. I was merely a thing to be patronised or demonised. In the UK is a debate on whether to lock up people with severe personality disorders, even if they haven't committed any crimes. This idea appals me. I'm not unconscious of the fact that this could have been applied to me. The opportunity to change for the better and mature could well have been stolen from me. I could have been locked up for having the history of an abused child who didn't know how to handle it. Better care or treatment is not deemed worthy of pursuing, but locking people up is. By better treatment I mean more than just having medication to deal with mental distress, like psychological therapies or social support. I'm sure pharmaceutical companies have a hand in policy making. The percentage of murders committed by mentally ill people is minute. You are more likely to be killed by someone coming out of a pub, but no one is saying ban pubs, even though alcohol does an enormous amount of damage to society. This says a lot about society's spurious attitude and ignorance towards mentally ill people.

For the same reason I liked Lego as a kid, because you can only build with it, I like words, the poetry of the catatonic. So I've kind of turned myself into a guerrilla artist: I write books, poetry, scripts, songs, short stories, journalistic articles; I paint, I draw, I act, I sing, I make music; I'm a photographer, I'm a film-maker, I'm a small press publisher, I'm a T-shirt designer, a book designer, a web designer, a graphic designer. Need I go on? Yes, I do need to go on. It's a do or die situation. I use art to hold together a life grown too large.

I tried to make sure my soul and my heart shaped my life and not the habitual responses my early life produced. I pushed myself and challenged myself. I saw giving into fear turns every moment of your soul into a cesspool. You stagnate if you don't reach beyond your fears. Knowing that my social skills needed developing, I made the point of making conversation with people. I remember one time waiting for a bus outside Lambeth hospital with an old woman. I asked her how long she was waiting for the bus. "Half an hour. I've lived in this part of London for 40 years and it seems to me I've spent half of that time waiting for a bus." I laughed and asked her about her life in London. We talked for half an hour about families and living in London. When the bus came we continued our conversation on the bus. When we both got off at Brixton Underground, she squeezed my hand and said "Thank you for being there. I really needed that." That really touched me. I knew I was doing the right thing. I'm overcoming my social phobia by jumping into the deep end by giving talks and poetry readings; meditation and yoga relaxes. I bought a diary and made sure it was filled with good experiences. All the things I was scared of do, I just got up and did. The secret is not to think about it but just get up and do it. I joined my local Buddhist centre and went to some teachings. I spent a few weekends with the community at Amaravati Monastery. I went to a few Brixton Academy gigs with Placebo and The Dandy Warhols. I travelled more. If I felt fear creeping in, I would say to myself, "Do or die, no more procrastination." And because of this my creativity was a thing I could not shut off. I think I wrote about a million words in 2001, including 2 novellas. I started up a small press called Hole Books and published my first book 'Eloquent Catatonia', which has sold steadily for months. I learned about web design and created a couple of websites including one for Hole Books, which can be found at www.holebooks.co.uk. I returned to First Step Trust and began working in their print room, making Christmas cards, calendars and pamphlets, learning skills useful to publishing. I joined almost all the mental health groups in

Lambeth and tried my best to help them out. Karate and swimming is proving to be great fun.

I added to my tattoos. My Mum began the trend in the family. I thought there's no way my Mum is going to have more tattoos than me, and I had my first one of a bird flying over a sun on my left shoulder. No more hearts on my sleeve, scars on my wrists, I was going to wear my soul in tattoos. You can tell which I had done when I was manic and which I had done when I was depressed. Around my right wrist is a smiling ghoul inside a gothic pattern. I think when people see it their eyes go wide and they think, oh-oh, and slowly step away, which is useful for job interviews. On my right upper arm is a death's skull also set inside a gothic pattern.

But on my good side – my left arm – is the aforementioned bird. Nelly Futerdo's "I'm like a bird' is my current anthem. Also on that arm is a bigger sun, and on my left wrist is the Hindu symbol representing the sound of the universe. I think I'll stop at about 20 tattoos, but then again on my Xmas present wish list for 2002 is a tattooing kit. I may take it up professionally. I joked that I could become a tattooed lady for the freak show. Kenny said I could also be the fat lady and bearded lady as well!

I'll get my own back on him one day...

Life was getting better for me, but I just couldn't forget about my Dad.

I twice arranged for him to go into hospital to detox as a voluntary patient. Both times he discharged himself. Finally at the prompting of my CPN I wrote my father's psychiatrist at letter. In it I said I had had enough. I said my father was killing himself and I had to stand there and watch it. I told her maybe it was better if I didn't help my Dad, so he would die quicker and be put out of his – and my – misery.

I thought the letter would have no effect, but thankfully it did. My Dad was admitted into hospital and this time he wouldn't be allowed to leave. Things aren't so clear cut any more about the mental health system. I was 100% against compulsory admissions. That was until my father was forced into hospital. It saved his life, I have no doubt about that. He would not be alive today if that did not happen.

He was in such bad shape he didn't even realise he was in hospital for the first 4 or 5 days. They got him out of his stinking clothes and made him have a bath. They did a liver function blood test and found his liver was severely damaged because of alcohol. After about two weeks he said he felt much better and wanted to go home. His doctor said no. One duty psychiatrist asked him if he had a problem with drinking. He made all the right noises and promises but when the doctor left he asked me to slip in a few lagers. I know from my own experiences, staying in hospital is boring and as my Dad was the youngest in the geriatric psychiatric ward he became restless. What was even worse for him, a few of the elderly woman wanted my Dad as their toyboy! So I accompanied him for walks outside the hospital. He asked me to go into a newsagent to get him some crisps. When I came out of the shop, I saw he had gone into the off licence next door to buy drinks. That upset me, the doctors had told him he would be dead within a year if he carried on drinking the way he did, and it made no impact on him whatsoever. I told him if he drank another drop, I would have nothing to do with him again. "He said you don't really mean that. You're too soft."

Fuck him! I wanted to scream. I didn't know what the right thing to do was. I went home and thought about it. I meditated upon compassion and realised compassion isn't being a doormat, it isn't helping somebody along in his or her self-destruction. Compassion for all beings means being kind to yourself as well. So I told my father how it was going to be. If he stayed sober, I would spend time with him and help him out. If he was drunk, I would not even utter a word to him. "Yeah, yeah," he said, not believing it. But I stuck by my word and held firm. I was glad when social services found a place for him in an Asian old people's home, where he would have restricted access to money and wouldn't be allowed it all at once, which means he has stayed sober, more or less, for about a year. But as I write this in August 2002 he is becoming restless and wants his own place again, which means he is clashing with the family again. We want him to be looked after; he wants to die in a thousand and one instalments we no doubt we also have to pay towards. Things will never be easy regarding my father, but life will always be bittersweet. Life can sometimes be a bad joke, but I've learnt to laugh at it.

My manic-depression hasn't gone. It still affects me day to day: I hear voices daily and I have to really push myself to do the right thing. I've still had serious episodes since my metamorphosis. The worst one happened in March of 2002 when I went to India. I planned a two-week stay there, hoping to visit Delhi, Bombay, Agra, Varanasi and the Buddhist holy places in Bodh Gaya. I booked an indirect flight with Kuwait Airways, stopping over in Kuwait City for a few hours. The airport there was spotlessly clean. As I sat waiting for my onward flight, I watched uniformed janitors push a mop or broom to and fro in the departures lounge, even when there was nothing to sweep.

On the plane from Kuwait to Delhi, I watched the night turn to day over mountains, deserts and lush greenery – it was one of the most beautiful sights I have ever seen – the sun rising, rising, rising, through golden clouds. However, approaching Delhi, the skies darkened under a thunderstorm. I wasn't able to see much of the ground, maybe a few twinkling lights. I looked at the in-flight monitor to see we were only a few minutes and miles from Delhi Airport, yet I had the distinct impression we were circling the city for the best part of an hour. The pilot confirmed this. He said due to bad weather conditions we were being diverted to Mumbai. The passengers protested. I didn't openly complain but I was worried about my room at the hostel.

Once we got to Mumbai, we were told the real reason for our diversion. A government minister's helicopter crashed at the foggy airport, killing all on board. At first we were told we'd only have to wait a few hours before re-boarding our flight. When it was obvious we were going to have to wait longer, the airline put us up in a local hotel.

The road from the airport to the hotel was dusty and dirty. The smell of cow shit pervaded the air. Palm trees and poverty is all I really remember of that city. At the hotel I ate and washed. I also made a phone call to the YHA hostel in Delhi where I booked a room to tell them what happened and to keep my room for me. The woman at the other end reassured there would be no problem. Yet when I did finally arrive at the hostel, they told me they had to give my room away. They asked me to come back in the morning where there was sure to be some vacancies.

"But it's 2 am in the morning, what am I supposed to do until then?" I protested.

They couldn't help me. I left the hostel swearing. I hailed a taxi and asked the driver to take me to an area with lots of cheap hotels. He drove me over to Karol Bagh. The 5th hotel I went into had vacancies, and I went up to my room to rest.

But the day's events had strung me out; I was unable to sleep. I could only shower and stare out

172

of my hotel window, which overlooked a grubby alleyway with a broken-down children's carousel on its side. In the morning I went to the local tourist office, which wasn't really a tourist office but a travel agents that tried to scam me out of my money. In the end I hired a driver/guide for the day to take me around the sights of Old and New Delhi. I went to Hindu temples, markets, the Red Fort, and Mahatma Gandhi's Darshan. That was the best part of my trip over there; standing over the eternal flame in the spot Gandhi was cremated. It was a very moving moment. After that the driver took me to a monkey park where I fed them fruit. The driver then took me to his local café where we ate a vegetable curry. I spent the rest of the evening walking around the city. I marvelled at scaffolding constructed out of bamboo rather than metal poles. I saw rickshaw and taxi drivers sleep in their cabs, clearly their only homes too.

The poverty and pollution was worse than I imagined, and I have a pretty good imagination. They both really hurt me, physically and mentally. Out of nowhere, I heard Gandhi's voice telling me to help the poor, so I began giving my money away, 100 rupee notes. I think I gave one old man beggar a heart attack. Soon other beggars saw what I was giving away and I was swamped by rags and outstretched hands and smiles. I gave away all I had on me. I don't know if it was the pollution, or not sleeping, or simply picking up a bug, I had developed a nasty cough. I staggered back to the hotel.

Luckily I hadn't taken all my money with me. I left some at the hotel. But I could see I didn't have enough for 2 weeks so I phoned my brother, Ken, to wire me some money over. Then I returned to my hotel to get some sleep.

It wasn't to be. Wedding celebration jangled outside my window for most of the night. An out-of-tune brass band marched up and down the alleyway for hours. I contemplated murder.

Come the morning and I was in pretty bed shape, physically and mentally. I had the headache from hell, a wheezy cough, auditory and visual hallucinations were having the time of their lives. I was also very hyper. I took the train down to Agra to see the Taj Mahal and other sights. I was so high I thought that I didn't need to take photos with my camera. All I had to do was think of the picture, blink my eyes, and the picture would show up on the film.

I returned to Delhi to pick up my money. Four days without sleep and too much sunshine, and I began to feel terribly homesick and pestered by thoughts that I wouldn't be allowed back into Britain because I was turning evil. I went to the Kuwait Airways office in Delhi to request an earlier flight home. There was quite a queue ahead of me. A few Europeans also wanted earlier flights home but were told there was a long waiting list - there was a lot of religious violence at the time. This didn't deter me. I told the lady behind the counter quite forcefully I had to go home *now*.

She said there were no spare seats available. I said, "All right, can you let me go up to the roof of your office so I can jump off and fly home that way?"

The poor woman looked horrified. Stammering, she told me to ring or come back in a few hours.

Well, I did. She managed to find me a seat on a flight that was going to leave that night. The flight check-in was 2am, but I booked a taxi for 9pm for the airport. It's lucky I did too. The taxi got into a minor car accident and had a flat. I helped the driver push the car to India's version of roadside assistance – 3 homeless mechanics sleeping on the roadside with their small dog. They tidied up the damage and replaced the flat tyre. I fed the dog popcorn as I waited. We got to the airport around about midnight.

On the plane home I was in awful shape – I was coughing and farting and hallucinating. Entering the tunnel leading to the plane, there was a sign overhead, which I'm fairly sure (I'm never 100% sure about reality) now said: Enjoy your flight. But *then* I thought said: Enjoy your death.' Okay I will. I thought the plane was taking me to heaven. It took me to Heathrow instead. The Sikh guy sitting next to me was a godsend. He could have complained about my behaviour or moved to another seat. Rather he tried to calm me down and told me stories about his family, and made sure I had a fresh supply of water for my burning throat. Talk about depending on the kindness of strangers.

How I got from Heathrow to Streatham Hill with a heavy pack, I don't know. I don't think I was even able to walk in a straight line. Once through my Mum's door, I was pounced on by 4 excited, happy dogs. It was so good to be home, I almost cried. Both my Mum and brother hugged me. My Mum was shocked how pale I was. She said, "I thought you were going to come back with a dark tan, but you've come back lighter than me!" She ordered me to bed, where I stayed for 3 days recuperating.

But I don't regret the holiday, and I don't regret my life. I just no longer identify with the illness. Yes, it's an annoyance but I've come to terms with it. It is part and parcel of my creativity. I'm even grateful to it for being a great teacher; it taught me how to write, it taught me not to be complacent about life. It taught me to be the person I am now.

I recently bought a bike - the so longed for bike from childhood. It took me a good few weeks before I got my balance. Suddenly I soared down the street outside my house without falling. "Weeeeeeeee!" I squealed. I just couldn't stop laughing.

EPILOGUE

This book I hope sets the record straight. I know honesty is atrociously painful. I didn't want any fucking secrets any more eating me up like a tumour. I learned the power of lies, how it superficially makes life easier to deal with. But in the long run it isn't really a life, but a story your soul only half believes. I thought I was unable to construct a viable narrative starting with 'once upon a time', and ending with 'happily ever after'. But this book isn't a suicide note. The overriding feeling I had when I finished it was to celebrate my life, and I *am* going to celebrate it.

I refuse to be ashamed about anything that has happened in my life, and I have no time for people who like to make others feel ashamed. But in writing this book, have I in turn disgraced or hurt my father? I just didn't want this book to be about a happy family full of lies. Although my siblings are doing the best with their lives and have large hearts, I see a certain pain in their eyes. I'm not going to pretend I don't see it.

I know the truth hurts for Dad, so much so dementia became a coping mechanism for a mind that doesn't want to know itself. I am sorry if this book hurts you, Dad, but I'm fed up with lies. I love you and want you to have peace. Please wish the same for your children.

Appendix

EARLY WARNING SIGNS OF MANIA

- **Sleeping much less:** That for me is the first sign of an impending manic state. I go from 8 hours sleep to 1 or 2, and sometimes no sleep at all. And even if I do manage shut my eyes, I dream more than sleep. The mind has so many ideas and preoccupations it tells me life is too short for sleep and there's too much to be done. You feel the whole world depends on you. Any kind of rest feels like a straitjacket.

- **Others seem slow:** when you're high, the whole world feels interminably slow. I get frustrated and angry with my family for sitting down and watching TV, I get irritated at them for not having an agenda to change the world, I am gob smacked when they can't do the housework in less than 5 minutes. It seems to me the whole world is trying to walk through water whilst I'm soaring in the air.

- **Making lots of plans:** I could fill up a small notebook a day with plans and ideas. At the moment these are my plans: write and publish 5 books simultaneously, do a parachute jump for charity, do voluntary work for 15 different organisations, set up a t-shirt business, train hop across Canada, climb a mountain, paint a picture, join a drama group, make a film… need I go on?

- **Spending too much money:** I'm in debt thanks to thinking I could save the world though my credit card.

- **Feeling superior:** I do have phases when I look upon the people around me as peasants in my kingdom, extras in my drama.

- **Dangerous driving:** I don't drive thankfully. I think if I did I would probably take the car out for a spin and end up in Russia.

- **Increased appetite:** I've got an arse you can rest your pint on.

- **Doing several things at once/ difficulty staying still:** My mum and sister do things in a linear fashion, one thing after another. For example, they drink a cup of tea, then they do the ironing, then they watch TV. I can't see why you can't drink your tea, iron your clothes, watch TV, write a poem, make phone call, do some exercises all at the same time.

- **Irritability/ easily angered:** why don't you people just leave me alone! Stop getting in my way!

- **Speeded up thought:** thoughts stumble over each other to be the first one out of your head. Soon enough they stop making sense.

- **Inappropriate behaviour:** hugging grannies at bus stops because they look cute or grabbing someone's arse is inappropriate, I'm told.

- **Unnecessary phone calls:** Thankfully, I haven't had a problem with that. But only because I thought my phone was bugged.

- **Very productive/ increased creativity:** I wrote over 100 poems in a week, a novella in less than a month. I think in over a year I have written over a million words.

- **More sexually active:** it takes all my willpower not to jump on some poor guy or girl. Being bisexual means the whole world is there for me.

- **Inability to concentrate:** It sometimes takes me an hour to read just one page. Shopping lists turn into suicide notes. Sitting through a film is torture.

- **Writing pressure**: sometimes I can feel I can write a novel in a day.

- **Surges of energy**: amphetamines are smarties compared.

- **Pressures of speech**: Usually I am very economical with speech, but being manic I will talk about everything that comes into my head, jumping erratically from subject to subject. I know I'm doing this when my talkative sister tells me to shut up.

- **Increased alcohol consumption**: I'm tea-total so this hasn't been a problem.

- **Taking on too many responsibilities**: this pretty much comes under **doing too much.**

- **Sensitive to noise and distraction:** how a haemophiliac feels in a razor factory is how I feel walking down a busy street.

WARNING SIGNS OF DEPRESSION

- **Reduced interest in activities**: Everything seems pointless, even thinking takes too much out of me. Sometimes the mind goes blank so you can't do anything. You think: I can't do anything right so why bother. Difficulty doing things because you're moving and thinking slowly.

- **Indecisiveness**: An ordinary shopping trip can take hours, because you can stand in the aisle debating whether you would regret buying three apples instead of two.

- **Feeling sad or unhappy**: Life sucks. Everything you look at gives you pain and a reason to commit suicide. Darkness surrounds you like a caustic fog. Despair and hopelessness are just another name for your thoughts.

- **Irritability**: noise, colours, movement are wrapped in razors. People annoying the fucking hell out of you just by sitting there.

- **Getting too much (hypersomnia) or too little (insomnia) sleep**: the spectrum goes from 2 hours to 22 hours. I have know others who have slept for days and kept a bottle with them to urinate in, it was that bad.

- **Loss of**, er, what was it again… that's it - **concentration**.

- **Increased or decreased appetite**: You mean I have to swallow after I've chewed my food – fuck that! OR: I could eat till I burst. I wish I would fucking burst

- **Loss of self-esteem**: I can't do anything right, I'm fucking useless, I deserve the worst for being so pathetic.

- **Decreased sexual desire**: sexual organs go into hibernation.

- **Problems with memory**: ironically I've forgotten what memory problems I had.

- **Suicidal thoughts**: the pain of depression is so eviscerating, you know waking up to a new day is waking up to a new hell. So what's the point, you might say, if I'm going to feel this for the rest of my life, I may as well die.

- **Crying uncontrollably and/or for no apparent reason**: you feel so helpless, the tears just come. It doesn't even need to be preceded by a thought or emotion.

- **Lack of energy and feeling tired**: getting up to go to the toilet is so much fucking trouble, fuck it, man. You just can't be bothered to do anything. Even thinking about doing nothing takes too much energy

- **Speaking/ thinking slowly.**

- **Hypochondriacal worries; fears or illnesses which prove to be psychosomatic**: I thought I had all sort of life-threatening diseases. I felt so awful I wished I *did* have life-threatening diseases.

- **Feeling dead or detached**: it's being in a waking coma inside of a glass cage. The world stops being real.

- **Hallucinating**: cooeee, it's only the devil talking. That's when it starts getting really bad.

To improve my health I needed the following:

- **Medication:** the one that suited me and had the least amount of side effects possible. I still have an ambivalent response to my medication. After many years of chopping and changing medication, I finally found one that helped me – Quetiapine, even if it was one of the reasons I had my termination. Although I feel extremely uncomfortable about that and the way pharmaceutical companies test on animals and shape mental health policy, I have to acknowledge the drug gave me my life back. Yes, I have tried to stop taking the drug to see if I no longer needed it and found the psychosis was still there

- **Good housing and social support:** When I finally got a good place to live and had my benefits sorted out, and help with my Dad, the relief from stress was palpable. I noticed this in others who've had mental health problems and finally improved their housing or home situation, how it changes their personality for the better. I can positively guarantee anyone who has been discharged from hospital and put in a shitty little bedsit with little human contact, or back into a violent home, **will** relapse.

- **Learn and practice relaxation techniques**. This is where my recovery began. Only a few months of yoga and meditation and everyone, and I mean everyone, noticed the difference. I could no longer believe in my depression.

- **Reduce stress as much as possible**. Stay away from stressful people, which meant I had to be firm with my father about how much I could see him.

- **The most important one:** belief in oneself. The things that have happened to me don't make up my soul. How I respond to these things makes up my soul. Are the only thoughts in your head of the bitter people who are too scared to live and what they think of you? What a waste. I realised I was responsible for my life – no one else. Blaming other people is a convenient excuse. Does it help you? Does it help the person you're blaming? Life's too short. Do you want on your gravestone 'I believed the bullshit so I didn't bother to live'?

- **Last but not least:** learn to laugh at yourself. Being human is an absurd and ridiculous career. The world is full of laughter – yours hopefully...

Chipmunkapublishing

The Mental Health Survivor's Publisher

ISBN09542218 2 6

Order online or write a cheque made payable to Chipmunkapublishing for £12 and send it to Chipmunkapublishing, PO Box 6872, Brentwood, Essex, CM13 1ZT.

WWW.CHIPMUNKAPUBLISHING.COM
Read first chapter for free.

World Is Full Of Laughter

By Dolly Sen

The acclaimed autobiography on Manic Depression/ Schizophrenia and child abuse.

Order online or write a cheque made payable to Chipmunkapublishing for £12 and send it to Chipmunkapublishing, PO Box 6872, Brentwood, Essex, CM13 1ZT.

ISBN 0 9542218 1 8

WWW.CHIPMUNKAPUBLISHING.COM
Read first chapter for free.

The Naked Bird Watcher

By Suzy Johnston

The eagerly awaited autobiography on manic depression from our first female Scottish author.

Order online or write a cheque made payable to Chipmunkapublishing for £12 and send it to Chipmunkapublishing, PO Box 6872, Brentwood, Essex, CM13 1ZT.

ISBN 0 9542218 3 4

WWW.CHIPMUNKAPUBLISHING.COM

Who Cares?

By Jean Taylor

An autobiography on manic depression from a survivor and carer.

Order online or write a cheque made payable to Chipmunkapublishing for £12 and send it to Chipmunkapublishing, PO Box 6872, Brentwood, Essex, CM13 1ZT.

ISBN 0 9542218 5 0

WWW.CHIPMUNKAPUBLISHING.COM

The Necessity of Madness

By **John Breeding**

Order online or write a cheque made payable to Chipmunkapublishing for £30 and send it to Chipmunkapublishing, PO Box 6872, Brentwood, Essex, CM13 1ZT.

ISBN 0 9542218 77

WWW.CHIPMUNKAPUBLISHING.COM

Poems of Survival

By Sue Holt

Powerful poetry of a manic depressive battling for survival. Extremely moving and honest.

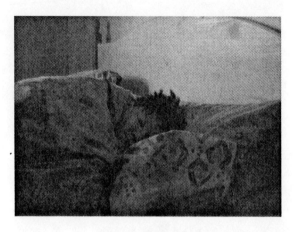

Order online or write a cheque made payable to Chipmunkapublishing for £12 and send it to Chipmunkapublishing, PO Box 6872, Brentwood, Essex, CM13 1ZT.

ISBN 09542218 9 3

WWW.CHIPMUNKAPUBLISHING.COM

Chipmunkapublishing

PROMOTING POSITIVE IMAGES OF MENTAL DISTRESS

THE MENTAL HEALTH SURVIVOR'S PUBLISHER

WWW.CHIPMUNKAPUBLISHING.COM

ADDRESS DONATIONS TO CHIPMUNKAPUBLISHING AND SEND TO:

Chipmunkapublishing
PO Box 6872
Brentwood
Essex
CM13 1ZT

Printed in the United Kingdom
by Lightning Source UK Ltd.
9691300001B/4-21